"With its accessible format, and the power of many male voices speaking from direct experience, *Speaking Our Truth* offers both a poignant invitation and essential support. This book will assist male survivors everywhere to emerge from their shame and isolation into healing. Neal King has made an important new addition to the field."

—Ellen Bass, coauthor of *The Courage to Heal*

"Brave and beautifully written, Neal King, with great courage, has found the delicate balance, offering the voices of survivors breaking their silence as well as his own wisdom, warmth and encouragement. The book provides invaluable guidelines for exploration and recovery. It will be of immense help to survivors and should be required reading for therapists."

—Terry A. Kupers, M.D., author of *Revisioning Men's Lives: Gender, Intimacy, and Power*

"The bravery and honesty of the men who share their struggles and triumphs in *Speaking Our Truth* left one moved, proud and hopeful. The world is a better place for having this book and the men who created it."

—Mike Lew, author of *Victims No Longer: Men Recovering from Incest and Other Sexual Child Abuse*

"A splendid little book offering words of truth, healing and comfort. No man in this situation should feel alone anymore. I highly recommend it."

—Wendy Maltz, LCSW, author of *Sexual Healing Journey*

[illegible] for Speaking Our Truth

[illegible]

SPEAKING OUR TRUTH

VOICES OF COURAGE AND HEALING FOR MALE SURVIVORS OF CHILDHOOD SEXUAL ABUSE

NEAL KING

HarperPerennial
A Division of HarperCollins*Publishers*

HarperCollins books may be purchased for educational, business, or sales promotional use. For information please write: Special Markets Department, HarperCollins Publishers, Inc., 10 East 53rd Street, New York, NY 10022.

FIRST EDITION

Designed by Nancy Singer

Library of Congress Cataloging-in-Publication Data

King, Neal, 1947–
Speaking our truth : voices of courage and healing for male survivors of childhood sexual abuse / Neal King.
p. cm.
Includes bibliographical references.
ISBN 0-06-095058-7
1. Male sexual abuse victims—United States—Psychology. 2. Adult child sexual abuse victims—United States—Psychology. 3. Child sexual abuse—United States. I. Title.
HV6570.7.K56 1995
362.7'64'0973—dc20 94-38869

95 96 97 98 99 ❖/HC 10 9 8 7 6 5 4 3 2 1

To the memory of my
brother, Ken

CONTENTS

PART THREE
FACING THE EFFECTS:
CONFRONTING THE LONG-HELD FEELINGS

PART FOUR
THE HOME STRETCH:
TAKING CONTROL—RECOVERY, INTEGRATION, AND MOVING ON

ACKNOWLEDGMENTS

A number of people have inspired, nurtured, and supported the process of this book becoming reality. First and foremost are the contributors, brave men who have given us the gift of their own tender insides and whose stories can move all of us toward a greater depth of understanding and healing.

There are also those who mentored and inspired me by their courage, example, friendship, and encouragement: Mike Lew, Franklin Abbott, Charlie Wolfe, Corey Kidwell, and David McCall.

There are two very special women without whom this book could never have arrived into your hands: Charlotte Raymond, literary agent extraordinaire who was an advocate and coach in the earlier stages and who has become a friend and valued critic, and Janet Goldstein, my editor at HarperCollins, who believed in this project early on and whose wonderfully loving and encouraging expertise helped both to mold and to finish this work.

And most importantly there are those from within my own "heart family" who have, each in her or his own way, helped make this book possible by believing in it and in me, and I thank each of them deeply. They include my sister Sharon Adler, friends George Shardlow, Ken Pinhero, Leslie Cooley, Kristine Belnap, Christian Villegas, Nick Casci, and Thomas Michahelles.

FOREWORD

by Thomas Moore

C. G. Jung's theories about the "shadow" suggest an attitude toward the dark elements in our lives that is so contrary to modern tastes for mental health and normality as to be a profound challenge. Simply trying to get rid of shadow, he writes, is like trying to cure a headache by cutting off your head. Elsewhere he equates shadow with the *nigredo* phase of alchemy—a blackening of emotion and of the values of life, and with *melanosis*—a necessary soaking in the bitterly dark hues of psychic pain and confusion. It's one thing to read this alchemically inspired psychological literature with intellectual distance, it is quite another to feel it as one's own life spoiled forever, as an impossibility to relate to others now because of abuse in the past, and as utter disillusionment when one honored person after another has violated one's trust.

Yet, Jung insists that we have to try to find some way to live with shadow. Current ways of regarding sexual shadow seem hygienic to me and excessively personalistic. The focus is on how I as a person can deal with abuse in my personal history. Maybe the only way to live with shadow, without becoming either literally cynical or naive about life, is to see even the darkest actions first as communal, as expressions of society's failures and needs, and secondly as frustrated desire.

We individuals suffer the frustrations and blindnesses of the community or, again in the words of Jung, "the individual conflict of the patient is revealed as a universal conflict of his environment and epoch." Our entire culture has tried to create a way of life that doesn't fully embrace the demands deep in the nature of things for eros–for desire, beauty, pleasure, sensuality, and intensely rewarding sexuality. We favor the realm of logos in the form of information, training, explanation, understanding, analysis, application, and efficiency, while we neglect and suppress eros. We think we can get away with this one-sided, apparently safe way of packaging and controlling our lives, but in fact we pay an exacting price in the painful ways eros makes its inevitable appearance.

What can we do as individuals? We can't remake culture, and we can't protect our children from its significant failures. One thing the individual can do is tell his or her story with passion, with stark plainness of detail, with rage and fury unrepressed, and with an artfulness that sends the story searing into the hearts of readers and listeners. We can sing this shadow so that it will be heard not only with the mind's perspicacity but also and especially with the heart's impassioned recognition.

Tragically, the modern world has forgotten the art of secrets. We don't know what to speak and what not to speak, where to reveal and where to conceal, when to bear our souls and when to respect our mysteries. Today people get on television and radio and bare their family traumas to listeners whose role is merely to indulge in broken secrets. Yet, as individuals we find it difficult to tell our own shadow-steeped stories. The art of telling our stories, knowing how and where to speak and how and where to keep silent, may be the key to creating a communal sensitivity out of personal tragedy. In a sense, our personal pain begs not for individual healing but for the creation of genuine community in which our emotional borders and our bodies can be respected. Perhaps in this way our suffering will be a route toward the discovery in society of its lost erotic life, revealing that individual pain has been a signal of social sickness, and that the blackening of childhood and family life that we call abuse is indeed an initiatory alchemical process.

But let us not turn this dark vision into a new plan for outwitting the soul's mysteries. This alchemy begins only when the darkness is felt and expressed adequately, when the individual finds the necessary courage to speak for the suffering soul, and when the community hears a message it doesn't like and truly finds some wisdom. Who knows how long we may have to endure our pain or how badly our families have to deteriorate before we finally see what is happening and what is needed? *Nigredo* is not an intellectual exercise, it must be felt and lived with a minimum of defense.

The soul always asks more of us than we would ever expect, and what is demanded is not that someone else change, but that we ourselves find a way of life that is in tune with the soul. If something deep in us and in nature requires a full erotic life—this, I suspect is the direction suggested by abuse—then we may have to give up some of the defensive postures we've taken in our mores and morals. We may have to reimagine our moralistic and structural views of marriage, education without love, an efficient world that easily dispenses with beauty, our total subjugation of nature, our secularistic politics, and ways of business that destroy communities and traumatize families.

The deeper our pain, the further we are from our hearts and from our natures. The more powerful and disturbing our stories, the more they can contribute to our necessary education in eros. Bitter juices play a major role in the alchemy of the collective soul, and just one of these unpalatable stories is worth infinitely more than yet another bland theory for explaining or preventing abuse.

It takes courage to tell stories of what actually happens, without the garnish of explanation. It also takes courage to read and listen to these stories without self-protection. For the odd thing is that there is hardly a more effective alchemical stew to be found than a well-told, heartfelt story of life as it is. A good alchemical vessel may be turned best not in a scientist's laboratory, a therapist's office, or an encounter group, but in a story paid for with personal courage and generosity of heart—the kind we can read in these pages.

THE SHADOW'S SONG

The power of story, of telling, of speaking truth is what this book is all about. As Thomas Moore writes in the foreword, "It takes courage to tell stories of what actually happens, without the garnish of explanation" and "it also takes courage to read and listen to these stories without self-protection." Speaking the truth is itself purging, cathartic, healing. The reader of *Speaking Our Truth* is invited to repay the courage of the men whose stories are offered here with the courage to read and hear and absorb their message. For the survivor, truth is central to recovery and healing, and the strongest ally of the spirit. Truth and spirit allow us to survive, and allow us to heal and become whole.

The fact that the stories told here are of men who were sexually abused as children is remarkable in itself. The women's movement and the very different ways in which gender is defined in this culture are significant factors in women having been sooner than men to tell their secrets, to express their horror, to find a voice for the pain and the injury inside. We men have believed that we are supposed to be tough, stuff it, keep a stiff upper lip, never express what we feel, and go on.

But with the understanding of the horrible truth that boys and men are also often the victims of abuse, perpetrated by both men and women, we come, hopefully, a step closer to the larger healing we all need to do. It's never been about us and them; there are no neat boxes or categories.

Speaking Our Truth offers a window into the internal experience of men who were sexually traumatized as boys. In the disquieting mosaic of poetry and prose of these courageous men, and through the remarkable drawings of Charlie Wolfe, the reader is invited into the largely hidden inner reality of the male survivor—as child and as adult. We witness a world that strains credulity, a world at once horrific, heart wrenching, infuriating, repulsive, and, paradoxically, profoundly rich as crucible for alchemical transformation: for healing, hope, and recovery. The hope is that we all, contributor and reader alike, heal a little bit more from the experience of this volume.

The evolutionary path of this book can be traced from my own experience as a boy who was incested by his father, through the many years of silence and levels of shame and paths to healing that in time brought me to tell my story to my graduate psychology classes when I discussed working with children and adolescents. I witnessed time and again the power of telling this story. For me, I heal a bit more each time I tell the story; I witness others emerging from their own shame and gaining courage to tell their stories as well. As I began to speak in more public and professional forums, it seemed important to invite other men into a collective telling of our stories, speaking of our truth, so that we and others might heal more.

So, the journey began. The writings that appear in this volume came from an intensive three-year international appeal for personal stories. The appeal was made through networks of therapists and organizations that serve survivors of childhood sexual abuse and through advertisements in journals and periodicals targeting male writers. Frequently, a note or letter would accompany the story or poetry or journal entries a survivor would send to me. They would often include comments like "I hope my story will help someone else on their way to recovery," "I wish you well with your project. It will be a gift for the thousands of thousands who need it. I *thank* you, " and "I am very pleased to see such a book written. . . . I continue to feel that there is no one who understands my feelings."

These stories are all the more poignant because we know how few of the total number of male survivors are represented here. Only a small percentage of survivors are able or willing to speak in such a forum as this book offers. Though few are expert or professional writers, each needed a certain level of confidence in his ability to express himself in English, in writing. There are clear implications and limitations of culture, class, and educational level in that one shared feature alone. The men whose words speak to you in this volume, just to have written and submitted their stories, also needed to have reached a certain stage of recovery and integration of their boyhood experience, reducing their proportion of the total population of male survivors even more. And, we know that many do not even survive their abuse physically, let alone emotionally and psychologically—and that many live out the effects of their abuse experience in prisons, mental institutions, as addicts, as perpetrators themselves, as spouse-beaters, and as child prostitutes.

We'll never know the exact extent of the male casualties of childhood sexual abuse. The contributors to this volume are the resilient few of a certain slice of the total population, and they speak from different stages of integration, recovery, and healing. I believe they nonetheless describe certain universal features of the male survivor's internal experience. You'll be able to follow some of us through several sections of the book, as the same voices appear and reappear. You can trace parts of our individual evolution in this process.

Many contributors have chosen to be identified by first name only; when more than one contributor has the same first name, they are differentiated consistently throughout the book by roman numerals after the name, as with David I and David II. A few have chosen to be identified by first and last name or by initials, and some have chosen to remain anonymous and are identified only as "A Survivor."

This is a reality we'd all prefer never to have existed. No child should ever have to be subjected to the experiences depicted in this volume. This reality is unspeakable—and yet, before we all can heal and before it can stop in the lives of children today, this reality must be spoken; it must be seen and heard. We know that many who are abused by others as children go on to abuse children themselves. Even for the many who don't, the man who suffers alone in silence lives with a constant barrier between himself and others. The man who begins to heal from these wounds begins to hurt less, inside and outside, himself and others.

The concept of shadow, discussed by Thomas Moore in his foreword as having both individual and collective applications, pertains in at least two different ways to these stories. There is the shadow place in the perpetrator's psyche from which the abuse springs. As Moore suggests, this can be an individual manifestation of the collective shadow, a tragic distortion and perversion of eros, given the overwhelming preference for logos at the expense of eros in this culture. Often the victim comes to experience the abuse as having sprung from, or rightly living within, some part of his own shadow: This is not the case, though the perception can be paralyzing and compound the feelings of shame and responsibility that complicate recovery from abuse.

The concept of shadow applies to the victim too, though not, in my view, in the Jungian sense discussed by Moore. Rather it applies in the sense suggested in this wonderful poem written by Tenzin Gyatso, fourteenth Dalai Lama of Tibet:

I call the high and light aspects of my being
spirit and the dark and heavy aspects *soul.*

Soul is at home in the deep, shaded valleys.
Heavy torpid flowers saturated with black grow
there. The rivers flow like warm syrup. They
empty into huge oceans of soul.

Spirit is a land of high white peaks and
glittering jewel-like lakes and flowers.
Life is sparse and sounds travel great distances.

There is soul music, soul food, and soul love . . .

People need to climb the mountain not simply
because it is there but because the soulful
divinity needs to be mated with the spirit.

Seen in this way, the experience of abuse casts a shadow between the natural union of spirit and soul, and inhibits and stifles a man's fullness of being and experience of self in the world. Healing for the survivor involves in part a sorting out of how shadow does and doesn't apply to him: It comes from the shadow of the perpetrator and casts a different kind of shadow upon his own psyche. His healing requires coming out from the cast shadow into the light of wholeness and internal union; the perpetrator's shadow is beyond his reach or responsibility.

Childhood sexual trauma, then, casts a long dark shadow between a boy's spirit and his soul, keeping the two from their natural union, and the developing person from the wholeness of being which could otherwise be experienced. This shadow is one of paralyzing confusion, lonely rage (often directed at one's self), suffocating shame and deep, unspeakable, private, seemingly unshakable pain. Within this shadow, the survivor can feel sentenced to a private nether world of secrecy, isolation, and powerlessness. Every shadow so cast has a story.

For men who experience sexual trauma as boys, this shadow is vigorously hidden and wrapped in collective shame. This book is the song of that collective shadow; it's a song sometimes of sorrow, sometimes of rage, sometimes defiant, sometimes profoundly sad. In moments it's a triumphant song, the song of a wounded boy at long last emerged from shameful isolation to become a whole man. It's the voices of many men raised together with the hope that with the singing of the song, the shadow will gradually dissipate, the mountain can then be climbed, the "soulful divinity" will be "mated with the spirit," and together we shall begin to heal and become whole.

We need to heal our hearts and souls, so that we might begin to have full, rich, loving lives as adults. Healing makes it better and makes us better, inside and for and with others, as father, son, husband, brother, lover, friend, worker, man.

This book seeks to help bring the heart and soul piece to the analysis, explication, and recovery aspects of the literature already in print. It reaches into the secret solitude of the survivor's heart and invites a voice to come forth from exhausting isolation into communion with the voices of others. It's a few courageous men speaking their truth, that others might find the courage to speak theirs as well.

Hopefully, this small book extends a hand to help the still-wounded male survivor (and those who love him) out of his secret shadow and into the light of day, voice raised in his own kind of song, joining the rest of us in our collective healing.

Speaking Our Truth is divided into several parts, each addressing a particular aspect of the male survivor experience. There is a progression, from the survivor's secrets to the ways in which the boy experiences the abuse to particular aspects of the abuse and the ways in which men respond to them. Each chapter suggests the various avenues by which men move toward healing and integration. At the end of the book, there is a list of suggested readings and resources for the reader who would like to explore this topic further.

A few thoughts on reading this book: We all need a safe place to confront and comfort and sustain and protect and forgive and love ourselves in the exploration of our own shadow. On my writing table, in my study here at home, there float two white camellias in a small crystal bowl. The flowers come from a shrub I planted a few years ago behind my home. I appreciate these flowers for two reasons: My mother, now many years deceased, particularly loved camellias and I continue to feel some connection to her when they bloom each year in late winter, and because they and the azaleas are the first to flower after heading out of the barren winter, harbingers of spring and heralds of hope. This is what our safe place needs to be for each of us: a place to privately and safely embrace that which we hold most dear and to tenderly nurture into life the issue of our healing.

Whether you're a survivor yourself or not, this is disturbing material to read. Please allow yourself some time to absorb what you read and reflect on your reactions. Allow yourself some company in this exploration—a friend, mate, therapist, or support group to witness your process and with whom to discuss and share the ways in which you find yourself affected. And, if you feel you need to do so, get some help to understand and integrate what you've read and what you're experiencing, including what might be newly triggered in yourself. This is important. It's okay not to do all the work yourself.

The list of suggested readings and resources at the end of the book can help direct you to sources of support and further exploration. You may well find that some passages will stand out and speak more directly and powerfully (even disturbingly) to you than others. This may mean that they are in some way similar to aspects of your own experience. Please allow yourself particular compassion in reacting to these passages.

We welcome you now to our stories and thank you for listening to them with an open heart.

PART ONE

HEALING BEGINS HERE

SEEING AND OWNING WHAT HAPPENED

CHAPTER 1

SECRETS

"HAVE YOU EVER HIDDEN A SECRET SO DEEP . . . ?"

The choice in regard to our secrets is relatively simple: We take power over them or we continue to allow them to take power over us.

Healing from childhood sexual abuse begins with telling the secrets, breaking the silence, finally giving voice to our private horror. It goes on for a lifetime, expanding and deepening each time we tell our stories, discover a new memory, give witness to another who struggles to emerge from denial or amnesia. But it begins with telling the secrets.

It's often tempting for a man to think, "I can handle this on my own; no one needs to know; I'll take care of this myself and be fine; it's no big deal." Wrong. It is a big deal. The secrets can kill you.

You don't have to be alone with this. When you're ready, you need to tell someone, someone you can trust. You'll be no less a man for telling your secrets.

We can pay a horrible price for not finding a way to bring our secrets out into the light of day, into a human place that's safe and protects us from harm. We're survivors both because we've survived the abuse and because we're still alive. Without being the least bit melodramatic, it's safe to say that many are less fortunate.

I always felt like they knew. I could never really be open because my secret might slip out.

C.L.

I have a second chance at life now just because I have survived this and can reveal and surrender these secrets to people who understand and care for and love me until I can love myself and have faith that God has something and someone very special in store for me now that this nightmare is finally ending.

Jim

Often the boy is threatened with harm to himself or others if he "tells" and is intimidated into keeping silent about the abuse.

I choked back my tears and went home, keeping silent as they told me I must. I don't know how long I remembered the incident consciously.

Joe

Denial becomes an important survival tool for us as boys. Paradoxically, as men, our living fully requires that we be free of it.

Probably the worst effect though is the raw pain that I have had to endure. When a parent has sex with his own child, it is perhaps the biggest betrayal that anyone can experience. I was absolutely cast out of my father's affections; I was alone. So I retreated to my brain. Denial is the skill that I learned very well in my household. And when faced with the awful reality of my father being sexual with me, I simply became very passive, and in the end, pretended that it hadn't happened. In other words, I "forgot" about it, for about thirty years. However, the truth was just under the surface of my memory, affecting every aspect of my life.

Murray

Drinking was my salvation. It kept me detached from my feelings. That substance eventually betrayed me and no longer worked. My crossroads was simply death or sobriety. My choice was simple.

John

Have you ever carried an undefined guilt in the ball of your stomach like lead (shot or poisoning) eating away at the lining, making you unable to swallow life as it is. . . . Have you ever hidden a secret so deep that it takes twenty years to find? Like coins behind the refrigerator; never moved until you leave where you have wallowed for so long.

S.K. Duff

Our secrets eat away inside at us. As boys, we form a relationship with our secrets. The boy who remembers but can't tell needs to find a way to live with this inside of himself. Some boys try to form some sort of life on the streets, often still as boys. Prostitution and the substances that often accompany and make this life possible frequently shatter a life even further. In the extreme, when we can't find a way to accommodate or tell our secrets, they can kill us.

Most days when I'd get home, or after dinner dishes were cleaned up, I'd go down to the basement and sit with my dog in his "house" under the steps. His name was Ralph, and he'd just lay there with his head on my lap and enjoy the pets or actually sit next to me and lick my face. He was the only person who wouldn't judge me for what was going on. I'd try to plot with him ways to stop it or would just sit there in disbelief. In my mind we'd converse about what had happened that day and Ralph would tell me it would be "Okay." I was glad I was the youngest of five kids then, because it was easy to get lost in the crowd. Nobody ever noticed I was gone and I needed time to pull myself together. I've always loved dogs because they'll love you back, no matter what.

Gene

My older brother died in the Spring of 1992. He was forty-seven years old. Medically, his alcoholism killed him. The fact of his dying was kept secret from him by a medical team that wanted to encourage his recovery. This final irony was consistent with the man's life. For much of his adult life, in military intelligence, he had guarded and kept the nation's secrets. He guarded and kept the nation's, the family's, and his own secrets with equal diligence, even as he tried to drown them. I believe his secrets killed him.

Neal

Joachim

by Jody

She said I was the most beautiful kid she'd ever seen.
Moist brown eyes so huge
they looked like
they could swallow you whole.

A mouth too juicy,
ripe and sexy
for any kid of ten.

They didn't think so.
They'd been using me
for pleasure
since I was five.

She was the only one I trusted
because I knew she'd lived the life.
When they were done with me
and threw me on the street to rot,
I asked her if the pain
would ever go away.

She didn't get a chance to tell me.
Someone else
answered the question
for her.

When they found my body
blue with cold out in the alley,
I was still wearing the sweater
she gave me.

It was the only time she ever saw me smile.

It's difficult to tell the secret, to ask for help. We feel weak, ashamed. Men, even as boys, aren't supposed to be victims or need help from others. The perpetrator uses and derives power from this reality.

When they got home, Mark's mother was in the kitchen, preparing a meal. She was a great cook. She didn't kiss or embrace Mark, only smiled and asked how the trip had gone.

"Oh, great, it's a really neat place. A beautiful campus," replied Mark, trying to get his parents to be confident and proud of their son.

"So we're all set for September!," piped his mother.

Mark knew he had just missed his chance to be helped.

[Later, while a student at the college he had earlier visited] Mark wondered if Gerry was doing this to other guys in the dorm, but could not ask anyone fearing that if it were not the case, he would be the subject of terrible gossip and mockery by his peers.

Mark

When we begin to tell the secrets to ourselves and others we've taken an enormous first step toward healing.

Through the process of disclosure, I was able to begin the journey through healing: to discover the person in me, to understand what was actually happening to me. I was able to begin to sort out the powerful emotions that lay buried within me for so long. Because the abuse was in contradiction of whatever was taught in the seminary about honesty, integrity, purity of heart, and respect for the individual, it made the journey even more difficult.

Louis

I'm thirty-two years old now and the abuse stopped fifteen years ago, but only this year was I able to forgive myself and recognize that I wasn't the one who had sinned. The guilt is amazingly strong and, in trying to deal with this entire circumstance, I was my own worst enemy. Now, six months after finally telling my family and closest friends—actually, I still haven't found a way to tell my father—the heart-racing and trembling returns with each time I tell the story. Sometimes I feel like it still controls me. It's my reminder of how powerful the feelings are that have been buried for over twenty years, and how these events have formed the view I have of myself and my participation/responsibility for the abuse. This has been the most damaging result, the most difficult feeling to shake, and the most important reason to seek help with my problem. Let me rephrase that, to seek guidance with my recovery. I decided not to edit that sentence as it originally came out, because it demonstrates the negative feelings that, because of abuse, come so naturally, and that I can only now recognize and correct. As every day goes by, I get more power over the abuse, and stop the thoughts and fears that have run my life. It was only through reading other stories like this in the several male child abuse books that I literally consumed, and by telling friends and family, that I was able to reverse the power balance between myself and my abuser.

Gene

There is a risk in my writing this piece. I thought about not signing my name. I thought about the just anger that some of my friends might feel—anger that I've faced in the past. . . . But my life has been made up of too many secrets for me to collude with any of them—even with those that might make my life more comfortable.

David I

CHAPTER 2

WHAT THE BOY EXPERIENCES

THE BOGEYMAN

As children we learn to blame ourselves and keep our trauma secret. As men we have to really struggle to find a compassionate understanding of what happened to us as boys. We were just kids!

Children are utterly dependent, powerless, and unable to understand adult sexuality. Innocence is an early and sure victim of abuse. A boy quickly learns that he can neither trust nor afford any form of vulnerability or any other "weakness" by which he might be considered less of a man and "more like a woman." He discovers that he must project and protect his "masculinity," which is sadly defined as being different from and superior to anything female. A great and tragic schism is born.

In order to heal this damaging rift, the wounded boy must be brought back tenderly and with forgiveness into our hearts as men, (the boy never was responsible for what happened). It means choosing as men to once again become vulnerable, as a strength, as an integral and cherished aspect of our masculinity.

When the child feels that the whole of the adult world has conspired against him, and there is nowhere to turn, he feels hopelessly alone, overpowered, and abandoned in his experience.

I am in a tent. It is night time. Someone is holding the back of my neck. Something heavy is on my chest. I can't breathe. I am choking. There is blue all around me. I am being buried by something blue. I am dying. The blue is the sky on my way to God.

Mike

I was always the last one chosen for sports, always the one who didn't fit in. I was so desperate for love or affection or approval, I should have had a neon sign on my forehead saying "victim."

Chris

Today I am a small blue thing, like a marble or an eye. I can hide in a corner or under a bed and not be seen. And I can watch, see, everything. I am much more than that, though. I feel something great, like weight. It holds me sometimes so I can't move, so I can't even talk. Or it moves me toward and away from things like people, love, and sometimes even life. It never seems to change. The weight is always there, even when I'm a small blue thing, like a marble or an eye.

Robert

When I Was Four

by Les

When I was four
I snuck up, hugged my father
He froze
A frightened cat
Eyes bulging out
Hair on end
Rigor mortis
When I was four
The music teacher stuffed his dick down my throat
His skin had the consistency of ice cream
I can still see the pores
When I was four
I'd wait smiling by the window for
Mr. ____ 's old green station wagon—
Recognized now as a '59 Ford—
To pull in the drive
Round head and taillights side chrome upsweep
His back seat pulled down to accommodate
Loose piano keys, guitar picks and strings,
Various sized mouthpieces and reeds
Discarded, broken parts of his students' musical instruments

Adult sexuality is foreign and incomprehensible to a boy. He has no point of reference in his own developmental experience by which to understand what is happening to him when confronted with this strange reality. Even physically, the difference in scale and development is bewildering and can be both terrifying and deeply confusing. The boy can be easily "flattered" that an older child or an adult would be interested in him. He is naturally predisposed to trust this attention.

Brad pushes the Scrabble board slowly aside. He pulls his pants down to his knees. His penis bobs in front of my face. It is bigger than mine, like everything else about Brad.

Eric I

One day I was walking near home when a neighborhood boy in his early teens asked me to play with him. This was new, unusual, and flattering to be befriended by an older boy. We went to an old abandoned car nearby. He said we would play "nuts and bolts." He pulled down his pants to show me how to play. At first he made some reference to his "nuts" and "bolt" and actually manipulated his penis with a wrench, and then asked me to try it on myself. I did, and though I was wary about this strange experience, I appreciated the experience of "playing with myself" for the first time. I think I managed a brief erection, but I was more fascinated by the older boy's adult-sized erect penis. It was quite impressive to me, so big and such a new sight. He encouraged my attention and had me touch it and hold it in my hand. Then he proceeded to masturbate, telling me how good it felt, which I could vaguely understand. Once, he tried to force my face to his penis and told me to kiss it, but I struggled away. It was a bit frightening, but mostly annoying, since I thought it was a stupid joke. . . . [Another time] he had another older boy with him . . . I decided my only chance to survive was to do what they wanted, even though their demands seemed incredible. . . . My jaws were tired and sore and I hated the world for allowing this kind of thing to happen. At the same time, strangely, I found this oral sex phenomenon curious, almost interesting amidst my shock.

Joe

For the very needy, and therefore very vulnerable, child, the abuse can feel like our one island of contact, touch, and attention in an otherwise desolate sea of isolation and need. The child who is not loved and protected at home is particularly vulnerable, at home and in the world.

Of course, for a tiny helpless child, any love was better than no love at all. Since so little love and affection was expressed in our family, I became a willing victim of my father's sexualized expression.

Murray

My mother abused prescription drugs. Sometimes she'd try to drive after taking codeine and alcohol. But mostly she'd just take several codeine tablets and pass out for many hours. She had absolutely no feeling of warmth or affection toward children. I used to long for someone to love me and show me affection. As a child, no one ever hugged me, or cuddled me, or said they loved me. I had no friends and no self esteem. I thought I was unlovable.

Chris

Frequently our healing as men involves a loving internal dialogue with our child self, who after all still lives inside of us. When we begin the dialogue, we discover the many ways in which we have long carried the abuse internally. We also discover that the child was never to blame.

That four-and-a-half-year-old child is still very strong, scared, ashamed, and discouraged within me.

Joe

The child within doesn't trust me yet. He doesn't feel I can, or will, protect him.

Nick

Sammy, that's what they used to call me. They, being my family, and anyone else who knew me. It was a name that, for a while, seemed to fit my personality. At least, that's how I see it, nearly twenty years later. Now, looking back to when I was eight, it's easy to understand why I had to insist on a more masculine form of my name.

When I picture a "Sammy," I see the epitome of myself as a child. A wafer-thin, walking toothpick with an unruly nest of hair resting anxiously on top. A jagged little creature, who would scurry off to the nearest corner whenever the hint of a shadow crossed his path. That was me: afraid, unsure, timid, and guilt ridden. At the ripe age of eight, I decided all that had to change. I would insist on being called "Sam" from that day forward. Much, much more manly . . . Sam. . . . Now that was a man's name. I needed that name. I wanted that name. And I took that name. Calling me "Sammy" from that day on meant you were asking for trouble. It meant you were calling me a pussy (I knew what "pussy" and "cunt" meant at that age, complete with descriptions and proper-usage instructions), and I would have no choice but to become a "trouble child" to prove you were wrong. . . . I would be forced to fight if you confronted me. As skinny as I was then, that would prove to be a monumental task, and one that would lend a good share of my visible scars. Later, it meant that I would have to become a drunk before I was twenty-one. And, of course, I would have to sleep with as many women as possible.

I'm still "Sam." Probably always will be, although calling me "Sammy" isn't an insult to my masculinity anymore. Sammy, of course, is still in me, somewhere; lost when I'm lucky. He remembers, though. Remembers well.

If you are a man, and you bump into me on the streets, let's play it safe, at first . . . call me "Sam."

S.E.

ADULT SELF: "Yeah," I said. "I just wish I would have done something to stop everything from happening."

CHILD SELF: "What do you mean?"

ADULT SELF: "Well, you know. The stuff with Mother. The stuff with Brad. I wish I would have done something to keep it from happening."

CHILD SELF: "Like what?"

ADULT SELF: "I don't know." I thought for a minute. "I just took it. I wish I would have stopped it all. The yelling, the hitting, the stuff with Brad. You know."

CHILD SELF: "But how?"

ADULT SELF: "I don't know! I'm not angry at you," I said quickly. "I wish I'd have been stronger. I wish someone would have walked in on Brad and me.

> Someone. I wish someone would have been there. Some kind of adult, someone who would have stopped it, or at least said to me, "It's all right. It's not your fault."
>
> *Eric I*

Especially when a boy's parents and, to a lesser but nonetheless extremely significant degree (particularly if the parents are not available as protection), other powerful adults in the boy's life, are his perpetrators, what is he to think? How is he to reconcile the impossibility of those upon whom he is most dependent willingly seeking to harm him?

I was taught to honor and obey my parents unconditionally. I felt envy for my peers who were beaten by their fathers and eventually retaliated and fought back. That must be such an empowering feeling to slay your dragon. Maybe my father wouldn't seem as powerful if I at least broke his nose. My basic role as his child was to comply with whatever was dished out. It would have been disrespectful, impolite, a commandment infraction, and just plain wrong to do anything but submit. I have the same tapes regarding my mother. She was his partner in crime. . . .

My mother was sometimes loose with her hands but she was definitely the lesser of two evils. Neither one of them felt safe, but with my mother, things were more consistent. These people were my higher power and their behavior must have been normal. What did I have to compare it to? Why would parents do something that wasn't in the best interest of their children?

John

I recognize now that the only way for a second or third grader to deal with the enormity of the situation is to ignore it, think about anything else, find some other activity to distract the mind. Fortunately for me, I chose schoolwork and prayer. Ironically, some of the most deeply prayerful times in my life were lying on my back inside the rectory while my pants were being pulled down. I was praying to God for the ability to understand why this was happening, sensing no answer to that, praying for it to stop. I settled for trying to concentrate on the crucifix attached to the wall above the door while he climbed on top of me. I remembered the classroom religion lessons stating that God sees all and everything that happens has some message from which to learn and grow. It's hard to understand the message when God's messenger is performing fellatio on you. . . . I can't remember the exact words, but I also think he told me nobody would believe me, because that night I dreamed that I did tell my mother and we had to go to court. There I was standing before the judge holding my mom's hand, who already didn't believe me, and there he was (in uniform for the public appearance) telling the judge I just got confused because he was always rough-housing and wrestling with the kids. Why would the judge believe a little kid over the pillar of the community? I was convinced that if I ever did tell anyone, I would be the one going to jail. I decided to just forget about it and next time I would have to be smarter about stopping him or just staying out of reach.

Gene

The boy quite naturally believes it's his fault and finds numerous ways of trying to understand what has happened that reinforce this belief. The perpetrator relies on this inclination of the child.

A simple question: How was I coerced by my perpetrator? (Maybe answering will prove it was not my fault.) The answer is a "mixed bag of techniques." And yet, somehow, for each answer, I can turn it around to being my fault. . . . I should have told someone. . . . I should have stopped him. . . . I should have yelled. . . . I should have . . . , [but I thought]

- your parents will disown and abandon you if they find out . . . and you'll have only me to take care of you
- I will do the same to your sister (four years younger) if you don't do it with me
- let's play doctor (then it would turn sexual and, since I was always the doctor, he'd tell me I was in charge and it was my fault things got out of hand)
- his social status (he was a servant in our household) was used to make me believe that I was in charge and that he had no choice but to go along with my wishes
- the slaughter of innocent animals (baby chicks, turkeys, chickens, rabbits, ducks) to assert his power . . . making it clear that the same could be done to me (e.g., throwing chicks off the balcony and then retrieving them to make chicken soup . . . all while I watched)
- occasional beatings and other physical abuse (either administered by himself or others . . . he acted as perpetrator and—at the same time—"savior")

I was only five to nine years old at the time. . . .

Nick

The boy can only use the ways of understanding the world he has developed so far to comprehend the abuse experience. He translates the abuse into his own childhood systems of understanding.

"Don't turn the lights out, Mommy, the Bogeyman'll get me," the boy pleaded as she was tucking him in.

"Oh, Jimmy, there's no such thing as a Bogeyman," she growled in reply.

"Yes there is, Mommy. He lives in the closet by the head of the stairs."

"Ohhhhhhhhh," she said gruffly, "there's only your toys and junk in that closet and you know it."

"Pleeeease, Mommy," he pleaded with a touch of panic in his voice, "please just check and see before you go downstairs."

"Jimmy, you've run me ragged all day long and I'm tired. Now you just forget all this nonsense and go to sleep." And with that she tucked him in, snapped off the overhead light, and went downstairs.

Jimmy

She then asked why I had never told her, that she would have killed him if she had known. I told her that was not true, that I had told her many times and many ways. It is hard to explain sex when you don't know what it is. When a child says he does not like his father, when he grows suddenly fat or lies or steals or rages or withdraws or runs away, he is telling the best way he can. I reminded my mother that her answers to any of this had been punishment and declarations of how much my father loved me. I told her that I never remembered her ever talking with me. She said she couldn't remember either.

Mike

It is the fortunate molested boy who finds a trustworthy adult who can see, hear, soothe, and protect him. This kind of presence in the boy's life can be extremely healing, life saving.

A trusting family, a supportive working environment and a heightened social awareness in our country [Canada] about the impact of sexual abuse toward children, made it possible for me to retrace the journey I had begun long ago. . . . I was fortunate enough during those years to find and courageous enough to disclose to one of the elder priests the sexual abuse. He listened to my troubled heart and understood; perhaps he understood pain because he suffered from Parkinson's disease. I felt understood.

Louis

Feeling and being understood in the actuality and reality of our experience as boys is vital to our healing as men. Each of us has to undertake this task in our own insides. When we're fortunate as boys, we've had the comfort, understanding, and support of another person somewhere along the way; as men, we still benefit greatly from finding this witness to our early experience.

CHAPTER 3

MEMORIES

"I BURIED MY MEMORIES FOR DECADES"

Many men never forget their sexual abuse as boys, or they remember in their minds and forget in their hearts. Other men find themselves as adults recovering bits and pieces of their abuse experience as boys. Healing includes remembering what happened to us as boys, in mind and in heart and gradually, each at his own pace, working to integrate what we remember and recognize the importance of the abuse experience. For the man sexually abused as an adolescent, this can mean recognizing that the abuse was in fact abuse. For the man sexually abused as a younger boy, this can literally involve remembering something that had been long out of conscious memory.

Memories come in many forms. We can experience body memories, feeling memories, or visual/cognitive memories, including dreams. We never know how or when a memory may present itself, or what might trigger these recollections. In time, we learn to recognize when we are being triggered, that something in the present circumstances resembles strongly something in past circumstances that was traumatic for us. We often, with good reason, resist memory. It's never easy to feel, and acknowledge the con-

sequences of, as a man what we needed as boys to put away for so long. It is, however, important to do so.

As men we are strong enough to do what the child could not have done. The child needed to survive; the man has survived.

We keep our secrets, and avoid remembering, for many good reasons. At one time, our survival depended, or seemed to depend, on telling no one. Oftentimes, the reality is too much for the child to bear and contain. He needs to put it away for later, until the adult is strong enough to recover it, to remember and integrate it. They come in many forms, these shards of shattered memory, often triggered by something in the present. They are drawn by the strength that the man has now, the magnetic pull of the soul's desire to be whole once more. Sometimes there's a waking "flash," other times, something comes back in a dream.

Have you ever . . . remembered . . . the fear of a ten year old whose arm was held and burned on the face of a grill for threatening to tell. . . . Did you realize that that child is you? At his son's birthday party, the Nazi-like man burned you. Your sisters remember your fear of going away on your first overnight camping trip with this man. The other boys were all elated, but your sister remembers your curious fear. You now cannot remember how he touched you. The act of burning took the incidents away. The fire raged through the fields—burning the inner terrain of your experience black. In remembering you will be ready to let go.

S.K. Duff

I was about thirty-seven years old when I realized that the strange memory that would occasionally flash through my head had actually happened to me. It was then that I finally decided to go into therapy. I had thought as long as I can remember that something was wrong with me, and the realization that this memory was real gave me something definite to bring to a therapist.

Joe

Last week you shared [in therapy group] that your uncle had forced his penis into your mouth when you were seven. I have never heard you say that. It jolted my whole body. I felt enraged that this had happened to you. It upset me so much I couldn't even talk to you about it. I know I have this memory in me too. I can't let myself think about it.

Mike

Since my brother died, I've been flooded with childhood memories, things I've not remembered for years. Two came in dreams, one of a small boy wandering out of the darkness of his sleep, clutching a teddy bear, into the dim light of the living room, where he had heard voices. He stands puzzled in a doorway seeing his mother on her back in a chair, a strange man crouching over her as he pushes her skirt up and gruffly mumbles something to her. The boy stares at the man's erection, never in his memory having seen such a thing. . . . The other dream-memory was of waking suddenly as my father was fondling me, sitting bolt upright and then looking to my right and seeing my sister watching from another bed, eyes wide, also sitting bolt upright . . . and then going promptly back to sleep.

Neal

The Plague

by S.E.

Harboring recollections
Of comforting blankets being
Drawn away, exposing me
To the harsh Alaskan nights
And his sickening, grinning
Indian Blood
How I
Hate

Remembering
Sweaty flesh and
Abrasive hands, fondling
Innocence and
Blind mistrust, while
Wasted energy was spent
Pushing
Rolling
Squeezing
Crying, and
Wondering
Why

There was an
Evil shroud of
Secrecy
Blanketing the
Musky odors
Erratic breathing and

Moaning finale, before
I was wiped clean
and told to

Forget

What bothers me most
Is what I can't
Persuade myself to

Remember

The child always wants his parents or guardians to have known and understood and felt his experience, and to have protected him and kept him from harm. He wonders how they could have not *known, and, if they did know, why they didn't protect him and keep him safe. This is a great mystery to the boy, which often gets internalized by him as a sign that he doesn't matter, or that it is all his fault after all. This continues to eat away inside at the man.*

Of course, when the parents have themselves, one or both, perpetrated the abuse, this confusion only deepens. Sometimes the depth of the confusion can only be dealt with by not remembering.

I had a dream on the edge of wakefulness this morning. I was standing with both my parents, very stationary and calm. They both asked me about my therapy—how things were going, what I was uncovering, etcetera. I'm aware that I've been telling them a bit, without having actually been through it in the dream. Then I slowly walk through a single sentence. "As a child, I was sexually abused." I have their interest when I begin talking about childhood. They know about that. Their heads arc, bowed-ears perked to my words. They listen and with the word "abused" they even nod slightly, as if they understand or even knew already.

David I

The memories can be sudden and often bittersweet: intrigue, pleasure, and enjoyment mixed in with the pain, bewilderment, and horror. When the boy first experiences this range of reaction, it is shameful and very confusing—and a good reason not to remember. The eventual remembering as a man is very freeing.

Memory. He had blocked it out. The abuse at home as a kid. It was locked away into a great Fort Knox of horrors. At twelve, his mind went to the rescue. It walled off from his daily consciousness his horrific nights of ass-in-the-air, belt around his waist horsey style, again pulled into his brother's notion of the right size, ten inches less than it really was, learning to make his ass and asshole move just right to prolong forever the moment of fraternal orgasmic bliss.

He had blocked out the beatings that accompanied any resistance. He had blocked out the realization that he both hated and but also loved his big brother for screwing him, binding and corseting him. He had taken the torture and eroticized it. Then his mind lovingly locked off the evidence, the source of this now self-inflicted abuse. But, as the Berlin Wall had only a few years before, it came down.

Six imaginary TV screens were playing in his mind's eye, each another scene of Billy getting used, beaten, and screwed, as Bill bolted upright out of his sleep.

Eric II

In the winter of 1990, I avidly read newspaper reports of young men who had been sexually abused by priests and suddenly, as if the words were magic, I was brought to total recall. Rapidly, I relived the experience of fifty days at a summer camp, where I too, was sexually abused by the director of the seminary. All the frightening experiences of thirty-five years before, replayed themselves in my mind. I suddenly realized that in my deepest apprehension something very sad and traumatic had happened to me; that my life had since been one of bondage and that every move I made was an attempt to escape that bondage. Even my leaving the priesthood was a powerful statement about how exhausted I was to live a life of deceit. My whole being rose up in revolt against that within me and I felt the liberation from all this with an intensity unlike anything I had known before.

Louis

In my "Incest Journal" I sometimes have trouble believing the vivid memories that began to erupt without warning on 7 November 1991, as I was walking south on Seventh Avenue to meet a friend for lunch at a SoHo restaurant, of my mother having sexual relations with me. Right on the sidewalk I went into an altered state in which I saw my mother, naked, lift me on top of her in her bed and hold me there. I seemed to be dressed in shorts and shirt—it was summer and warm—and I could smell her powerful body odor, something that often repelled me as I grew up and which she masked with various deodorants (Mum, Arrid) and perfumes (Jean Nate, Obsession), the scents of which also turned me off. Then there was a subsequent vision of my mother sitting on the toilet and inviting me as I innocently passed by the open bathroom door to come in and touch her pubic hair, and amazingly I feel a tug of excitement in my groin whenever I recall these sexual interludes. The lure of the taboo?

George I

When, at any age, we try to surface the memory and tell someone—and "someone" can't or won't hear us—we often bury the memory with new resolve.

I didn't even know I was a survivor until I was thirty-one. I remember telling a shrink about the rape so I could get out of jail on a drug bust. The shrink just laughed at me, "So you got cornholed. Now tell me something important." That's when the memory went peripheral.

C.L.

I have one image of turning to my mother following one incident, with my hand covered with blood, stool, and semen (mother's medical words for these substances) and being told that I had gotten myself into a fine mess. I believe she has some idea of what was happening but did not care enough to stop it. Because she did not validate my understanding of what was happening and did not stop it, I buried my memories for decades.

Eric III

There often are parts of our experience we never will be certain about; we can only wonder. The best "circumstantial evidence" possible is not the same as knowing for sure. Though this can be a frustrating and difficult aspect of our healing process, it's important to learn to listen to our dreams and intuitions and decide for ourselves what authority we attach to the images that present themselves.

One time in my therapist's office, I had a memory of receiving oral sex from an older man, while I was a boy of seven or eight. I believe it to be my uncle. I saw the whole scenario from above. It was frightening. I felt numbness and left my body. It felt so wrong.

John

The dreams came again that night. Dreams that left me alone when I was alone, but now there was Mandy creeping around in the back of my mind with the rest of the things I was afraid of, making them real, bringing them to the surface, back from the dead.

There were hands all over me. The older boy, from the house on the corner. His friend. His friend's father. Their fingers, thirty of them, moving and grabbing, pulling on me, spreading my legs, my lips, holding my head to their groin. Their penises, three of them, rubbing against my skin, slowly, rhythmically. Down my chest, my stomach. The head of the father's, purple and swollen, the biggest of the three. His hairy hand gripping it, the veins in both popping out. My eyes watching the long thin roll of flesh pointing down just below my own penis and disappearing.

I know what comes next even though I look away. I start to feel the pressure, his hips pushing his penis forward, into me. And then the pain. It moves haltingly and then as if something had popped, it slides in fast, past the sphincter, burning, tearing at my insides. There is a weight bearing down on me. So heavy I can't breathe.

In my dream I hear the burning, hear it rip into me. I feel the searing pain shoot through my whole body and then everything is black. All I can feel is sound, breath moving through the air like a flock of birds, coming closer, their wings beating faster until the noise is unbearable. I cover my ears. But I cannot shut out the older boy's voice saying, "Come over and play. My parents aren't home. It'll just be you and me." I cannot shut these words out and I cannot shut out my delight that he picked me. Of everyone in the neighborhood to play with, he picked me. I cannot shut these things out unless I wake up. I do.

Robert

UNTITLED

by C.L.

memory has many forms

the blood is the first memory
it takes a lot of snakes
shedding skins
it takes a lot of sweat
and self-torture until
the memory comes
so familiar
left as a stranger
to my own blood

the second memory is a vision
the second memory does not die
many deaths
in this mirror I have
remembered that I have
infected my DNA
this should be somebody else's memory

flirting with madness
to solve this memory
of a young child watching
the sacred sundance.

Sometimes we make a kind of deal with ourselves: The mind can remember, but the heart can't. That way we don't have to feel what we remember. This is useful and adaptive for the boy, but an obstruction to living fully for the man. Both the mind and the heart need to remember.

The catalyst to unlocking these emotions was the pain and grief my wife and I experienced after she miscarried our first child. My first reaction was, "Of course the baby died, you don't deserve one." We decided to go to a therapist because we were dealing with the loss in very different ways. I was trying very hard to bury yet another bad feeling, forget about it, move on. She was needing me to suffer and share with her. . . . My strength in keeping a lid on my feelings had been demolished by my grief over the baby, and while I resented her at the time, I have my wife (and baby) to thank for making me get on the roller coaster of emotion, acknowledge my secret, recognize its recurring effects on my present life, and finally step out from behind the guarded shell that I had maintained. This year has seen greater highs and deeper lows than I have ever experienced, but while only partly through the process, I can recognize for the first time the true benefits of love and trust in a relationship based on complete honesty with each other and with myself.

Gene

I remembered that there was always a blue uniform. I can see the sleeves as a man's hands cup my screams. I am bent over a saw horse. It is like a cross breaking at my stomach, and the force of his weight against my body forces me to puke. We are in a garage. There is a concrete floor. I remember it being concrete, because my watch slammed against it and broke as I struggled. The floor is covered with newspapers with urine stains and kitty litter scattered about. There is some dried up cat shit with dryer lint hardened on it. The dryer spins ahead of me. It is loud. I can cry. I do cry. . . . But no one hears. It is not my father. It is not the Webelo leader. Webelo leaders wear khaki uniforms. This one is blue.

After having the memory, later when trying delicately to extract information from my mother to piece it all together she made the uniform color comment. There was one other father who worked with the scouts she says. He was an auxiliary policeman and always wore his blue uniform. He took you on newspaper drives in your father's absence. . . . Your father didn't trust him she says. Daddy didn't trust him with Momma alone—but what could he do to a little boy? A ten-year-old boy. There is silence on the phone.

S.K. Duff

The sense that I was raped anally is trying to surface. I am fighting that tooth and nail. There is much evidence and strong feelings pointing in that direction, but I can't seem to own that. If I own that, it makes it real. If it is real, I fear that I will go into "vegetable mode" and never come back. I hear that the worst is over. I chalk that up there as another trite slogan. The feelings can be so intense and real, it feels like I'm living this stuff over and over again. I wish there was a shortcut.

John

Only we can know when to trust what comes to us as memory. Others cannot decide for us what did and didn't happen to us. The dream image, or those which come to us in hypnosis, can register with a lesser degree of confidence than the memories we never lost or doubted. A court of law has a different standard of proof and evidence than we have in the privacy of our insides. We have to be our own authorities about what happened to us, listening to others' ideas and suggestions, but ultimately owning and believing only what we know from inside to be true.

CHAPTER 4

DOES IT MATTER?

"I ALWAYS THINK THAT MY STORY ISN'T REALLY WORTH TELLING"

Our healing takes another great step forward when we recognize that our stories (and by implication we ourselves) have value—that our stories are not only worth telling but need telling.

The abuse often teaches us to value ourselves so little, how can our stories be significant, let alone worth telling? For so long the child punishes himself with the belief that it was all his fault anyway, so of course it doesn't matter.

The man knows better and exonerates the guilty child by telling the child's story, freeing both the boy and the man.

The survivor frequently minimizes his experience, even as it continues to paralyze him emotionally in adult life. The younger boy who is abused quite naturally explains the experience to himself as having been his own fault, much as a child will blame herself or himself for parents' quarrels, a death in the family, or a divorce. The older boy blames himself for "letting it happen," after all, he reasons, he was big enough and old enough to stop it, and should have done so.

When the abuser is a sibling or another child close in age, it's tempting to dismiss it all as "we were just kids," and try to convince ourselves that there are no lasting effects.

In either case, the severely damaged sense of personal worth pervades the survivor's experience of himself and keeps him quiet about what happened to him. His story is always worth telling. It's very important that it be told, and heard.

I need to protect myself from reacting to comments like "just get over it." I can't "just get over it." I wish I could. Only other men who have survived what I survived truly know this. I feel like I could write forever. I also feel like I must be cautious in what I write—careful not to give too much away and thus identify myself. It's the guilt and shame interfering again!

I was only five when the abuse began, and yet I can't get beyond the belief that I was responsible for what happened. As you read this, I feel that you'll judge me and determine I am a bad person and that you'll dislike me (or be disgusted with me for what I did).

Nick

It is difficult to believe that I am writing my story of abuse for possible publication. It is also hard to own that this is my story. I go to great lengths to ignore the pain and terror that is in my history. I often wonder if I'm making it up or have concocted these distortions by having an active imagination.

John

I always think that my story isn't really worth telling. I've read a lot of books and heard a lot of really awful stories about child sexual abuse . . . so it is easy to minimize my experience. Even to say that nothing really that bad happened to me. I guess it's how you decide to look at it. I have all of the scars of childhood sexual, physical, and emotional abuse. I don't know if I'll ever be able to trust anyone enough to have a good relationship. Loving and nurturing. Because that is what I've always wanted, as long as I can remember. But it is something that continues to elude me. I was just a little boy, I think about eight years old. And the abuser was my brother, who was only eleven.

Jeff

You can sense his presence before you feel him. You roll up in a ball. You feel a strong, powerful hand and go rigid. You shake. Slowly, you are pried open. A body lays down across you and a wave of pleasure erupts, emanating from the loins and turning you electric. (You cry at this sentence.) That initial connection can swallow you up. It is a moment, only a moment, of total pleasure. Then it is horrible. There is a smell and the grinding pressure of a body too big and too heavy on you, a frightening body that hurts if you fight. You feel dirty and exposed and empty and used. The hand moves over your mouth and nose. Suffocation is always a part of this, or gagging, and the fear of death. Death terrifies you.

Death is synonymous with being separated from your mother. There is weird breathing, then departure. Your spine is rubber. There is no strength in your limbs. You hyperventilate into your pillow. You are nothing. You feel shame for being alive.

Mike

I'd feel so guilty afterwards that the shame was easier to bury than to cry about so I wasn't able to cry about the abuse until this year. I became an expert at burying feelings and controlling emotions. The good news is that it helped me survive. The bad news is I buried all feelings, so I lost the good ones too. I really don't remember any feelings about birthdays, family vacations, good report cards, or any of the normal experiences about growing up. I remember some of the actual events, but not with any depth or clarity. I was so afraid of what people would think of me if they found out what was happening. I guarded every action, every word, to be sure it would not indicate in the slightest way that anything was amiss. I was much happier maintaining a solid line on emotions, not wanting to feel anything below the "acceptable" level. That lasted until this year. I was never on any kind of emotional roller coaster, where bad came with good. I stayed off the ride, sat on the bench and waited for everyone to come off. I had no idea what I was missing.

Gene

The biggest struggle for me has been around believing myself. Even after over three years of feeling that I was abused, I still question the veracity of the memories I've retrieved in hypnosis. It is like visiting the D-day beaches (which my lover and I did several years ago), not knowing what happened there. Just seeing the giant bomb craters, sensing the ghosts. Did bombs really fall here, I wondered, the physical evidence mostly gone. Only the long term aftermath remained, and I felt tears in my eyes. . . . And just sometimes it's a comfort to know that even after a devastating bombing where thousands of lives were brutally crushed, it wasn't long before life sprouted up from the ashes, and the survivors put up signs and monuments to tell others what really happened.

A Survivor

PART TWO

FACING THE REALITY

What Happens and the Forms It Can Take

CHAPTER 5

THE MALE ABUSER

"WHEN HE WAS DONE . . . "

Any boy quite naturally gives great power to his male role models: mentors, teachers, coaches, older brothers, uncles, ministers, and dads.

When a role model is also an abuser in the boy's life, an essential part of his identity formation, of learning how and who he will be as a man, is distorted.

Before the survivor can fully enter into his own identity as a man, he must find a way to exorcise the imprint of his male perpetrators on his own male identity.

Healing requires that we learn to trust and respect ourselves as men; to win back for ourselves exactly those things which our male perpetrators' betrayals taught us not to feel for them as men.

In order to figure out how to be as men ourselves, as boys we need and deserve to have powerful and positive experiences with the adult males in our lives. Incest and molestation are the opposite of what boys need and expect in relation to these men. We are very confused by these activities, and they complicate our developmental process enormously. As male survivors we are frequently robbed of the opportunity to model our forming identities after respected men.

Why didn't dad ever ask me to play ball?
Dad gave me baths.
Please don't.
Don't touch me there.
Down there.
Please

Les

I remember feeling dwarfed inside the dark confessional booth trying to come up with a couple of sins to tell the priest, and all I could think of was taking three cookies when my mom had said "only two," and lying to my dad that I had watered the lawn the previous day, when I'd decided to watch TV instead. I worried about remembering the entire Act of Contrition but thought things were sailing along when the priest decided to ask a few additional Sin-related questions. I remember only one: "You aren't touching yourself 'down there' are you?" My heart stopped; the nuns had never brought that up in religion class, and I certainly didn't think it would make it to the Sin List, since another priest had taught me how to do it.

Gene

Sammy was the boy that pretended to be asleep while his stepfather crept into his room late at night. The boy that didn't know grown men weren't supposed to suck on little boy's "thingys." The one who believed it was "okay," and it was "our little secret," even though something inside told him what this man was doing wasn't right. Sammy was the boy that discovered, too late, what "molestation" meant. He discovered the shame as well.

S.E.

I remember that I started listening for my parents at night to determine if they really did have sex. I would sneak through the house and try to listen in the dark. When I heard them, I always tried to figure out if he sounded more excited with her than with me. I wanted him to like her more. Then I felt guilt that I was inflicting this terrible punishment on my mother. I used to grab her and cry. She had no idea what I was doing.

Mike

My perpetrator was my father. For the longest time, I remembered a single incident which occurred when I was twelve—and the years that followed of fighting him off and running out of the house until someone else came home, determined not to let it happen a second time. I didn't tell anyone for years.

The keeping of the secret was encouraged by the fact that my father was a very bright man with many talents. He could be immensely charming and engaging, especially when he wanted something. Many saw him as a strong, even powerful and delightful man, and he had several good friends. I could see that for some others, he was even a positive influence.

It was as if I had been attacked by his "evil twin," which only I had ever seen, and was deprived of all the good in him. How could

I communicate this twin's reality to someone else? How could I even understand it myself? The tension between the two of us in the home was awful, and felt by all. He knew that I knew and that I didn't know what to do with what I knew.

Neal

The abuse can come out of nowhere and seem almost like it can't have happened when the boy and his perpetrator then return to their "normal" lives. The boy has no place to put this experience, no way to normalize it. Often he stores it in some split-off compartment of his mind and heart. It simply doesn't fit with the rest of what's going on around him, or even with the rest of his experience of the perpetrator.

My uncle took me to a park near his house and anally penetrated me under a tree in the winter. I was face down in the winter snow and the pain from his penetration was overwhelming. I could hear men (probably teenagers) playing Curling nearby. Curling is a Canadian game using brooms and there is a lot of yelling.

Roy

When I was four years old, my father sat me on his lap and let me steer his car. We drove down to the lake. . . . No one was there. He suddenly grabbed me by the groin and pushed my mouth over his erection. He was squeezing the hell out of my groin and gently moving my head up and down. He kept making bizarre gasping noises. I was scared to death. I was choking. His breathing made me afraid he was dying. I was afraid I was dying. When he was done, he shoved me, almost threw me, over against the passenger door. He didn't say a word. After a minute, he pulled up his pants and drove us home.

Mike

My father was a naval officer who, at the time of my abuse, had a division of ships under his command. When I was twelve, he invited me to spend a few days on his ship with him. I slept on the floor in his stateroom. This is where one midday, his face distorted with what I later realized was lust, he brought me to my first orgasm. I didn't know what was happening; it felt good in my body and not good with him. I was immediately ashamed and confused. He told me this was something I shouldn't do with myself.

A few minutes after he'd finished, we were sitting around the table in the officers' wardroom at lunch. He was the senior officer, and engaged in banter with the others as he would on any other day. It wasn't just any other day for me; I didn't know how or why, but I knew that something had changed forever inside of me.

Neal

Sometimes it feels good, but doesn't feel right. Sometimes it feels good at first, and then it doesn't at all. We can easily confuse arousal and physical pleasure with consent. A boy's natural need for closeness and affection, and the body's pleasurable responses to the abuse, confound the boy's confusion.

When the perpetrator is a parent or other loved adult figure, it can be a great shock to eventually let oneself see the truth. We lose the fantasy of who we wish the man had been to us; we gain an unwelcome but ultimately healing truth.

My molester, a man I'd known all my life, never forced himself on me. He didn't have to. He was my hero. When he crawled into my bed that first time on the night of my fifth birthday, I at last had his undivided attention. . . . It took thirty years to come to the realization that I'd been betrayed by a man I loved and trusted. It wasn't until I learned that my son had been molested that I was able to face the fact that I'd been emotionally blackmailed, robbed of an eight-year chunk of my childhood. By a man I still saw on a regular basis. A man with whom I still talked, laughed, hugged and shared meals. A man with whom, in an act of incredible denial, I felt comfortable leaving my son. Thirty years.

A Survivor

TEACHER

by Scott

At age twelve, I see you
standing next to me in
the school locker room,
giggling nervously, voice
soft in the dark. "Don't
tell anyone." Feel your
hand move down my body,
start stroking. Intake
of breath, then warm
shame on my stomach,
running down my thighs,
wondering if this is
right, knowing you
will be teaching me
algebra in twenty minutes.

Once we've been molested, we become vulnerable to revictimization, partly because we believe the perpetrator has all the power and we have none. This can compound and reinforce all the internal messages delivered by the original abuse, and deepen the attending confusion. Even as adults, we can fall prey to the same dynamics we experienced as children. We have to learn, often as men, what should have been our birthright, and was instead taken away: no one has the right to wield or exploit their power over us, in the sexual or any other realm.

It didn't take long for him to get at me again, and then I was locked into secrecy. Once, maybe, but nobody would believe I wasn't a willing participant if it happened twice.

Gene

When I was twenty I told someone for the first time what had happened to me when I was twelve. He was a man who had become a very important friend and confidant, a man who was also a psychologist and cleric.

Through a sad manipulation of his position and emotional power in my life, together with a desperate, misplaced expression of his own need, this man became my second perpetrator. It was ten or twelve years later, during personal therapy as I prepared to become a psychologist myself, before I told anyone again.

Neal

Our confusion about what has happened to us, and what it means to our developing identities can be significant and mistaken for what is our own sexuality apart from the abuse. This can become tragically interwoven into our sense of who we are.

We can find ourselves integrating the confusion from our abuse into our developing sexualities in a number of ways. We can be aroused by memories or situations which resemble the circumstances of our own abuse. We can imitate or repeat the behaviors we've learned from their being visited upon us. We can subject ourselves to repeated humiliation in sexual encounters parallel to the abuse experience itself, or find ourselves engaged in promiscuity or the reverse, a fearful abstinence from sex. It's important that we learn that we are not the same person as our perpetrator(s) and they are not us, even though their imprint on our lives can confuse and complicate our own sexualities a great deal. Healing requires that we know and feel this distinction in the depths of our souls.

I was born in Northern Italy fifty years ago. As it was customary at the time, my parents sent their two children to a boarding school with the intent that one day we might continue into the seminary and eventually to the priesthood. My parents were very religious and the church played an important and integral part in our lives. . . . It was during the summer months during grades nine and ten that I was sexually abused by the Director of the House, a priest. I cannot remember exactly how many times but it was over a two month period and always at night.

Two years following that summer, I joined a religious order and took the vows of poverty, chastity and obedience: the same vows taken by my abuser. I was in my sixteenth year then, in the middle of my adolescence physically but emotionally stunted. It still boggles my mind today!

Louis

Fingers as a Second Language

by Sam Ambler

Fingers is the second language I mastered fully,
feeling second nature. My first teacher
was my brother 5 years older. He would chase me,
tackle me, sit on me, tickle me, his fingers teaching:
this spot makes laughter, and here here too.
I would shout out loud between heavy laughing:
Uncle! Get off! Stop It! But he would only listen
to my fingers scrambling past his fingers
searching for his spot that taught the fingers language.

My second teacher was my neighbor,
Billy junior's father, 18 years older.
He distrusted words, the secrets they held and told.
When I was 15 his fingers caught my belt,
hauled me back, pried loose the buckle, his eyes
great magnets. His fingers grazed my pubic bush,
braided twice the hair, his fingers teaching:
this spot makes laughter (such different laughter)
and here here too. But my shouts were not out loud
the many times after, only for him, only him,
I guided his fingers.

That year he died flying a plane
that struck a mountain he thought was a hill.
I speak to him sometimes still
with my talkative fingers
wrapped around his favorite word.

The first incident of incesting was Jimmy's raping me. Over time I became his sex slave, he pimped me out to other cousins and guys in the neighborhood. I began sexual relations with my father at the age of ten and this continued until my seventeenth birthday. I was wildly promiscuous as a prepubescent, and over the course of many years have allowed myself to be raped hundreds and hundreds of times. I had no boundaries, no way to distinguish between intimacy (sexual and emotional) and being taken advantage of.

The second [recollection] is of me swinging on that clothesline pole, the end next to the back porch of our four-family house. I am pretending to be nonchalant while my cousin Jimmy is talking to me, mixing sexual innuendo with physical threats. He is the eldest son in his family, and the next two younger brothers (there will be two more, eventually), Billy and Dave, flank him on the porch. While they will not participate in Jimmy's sadistic sex games, they reinforce his authority. It is a terrible dispute of a sexualized, internecine gang war—my cousins are asserting their power over me. For you see, I live in one of the upstairs flats—it is a four family house and we are all first cousins on my father's side—and those of us upstairs must negotiate right-of-way passage across the side yard; it "belongs" to the downstairs cousins.

At the end of this confrontation Jimmy will take me out behind the neighbor's garage and force me to suck his cock. I am electrified with terror throughout this episode, one which will be repeated with many variations, over and over. . . . During my teen years we lived in a large house on the edge of a tiny farming community in a remote area of the country. All the while I was servicing my father (and having sex with some of his male sex partners), my mother was a "semi-invalid." (This was the term we were to use.) She was bed ridden much of the time, and it was my duty to take care of her and the household. I changed her bedpans, gave her sponge baths, cleaned the house, did the dishes, mowed the lawn, took care of the cats and dogs, tended the family garden. My sister was exempted for the most part because she was "too young." If I rebelled against the work or complained about not being helped, I was berated and slapped across the face, belittled for being "ungrateful" and for breaking that fucking Commandment.

Les

CHAPTER 6

THE FEMALE ABUSER

"I WOULD CUDDLE UP TO HER . . ."

Women are important models for developing boys as well, from whom we derive our ideas and impressions of how men and women relate as adults. Though researchers don't yet know what percentage of abuse is perpetrated by males or by females, we know that women and girls also molest boys.

There is a cultural message that says that the abuse isn't really abuse when it is perpetrated by a woman. Often the inability to trust, and its implications at all levels of intimacy, represent the deepest loss and one of the greatest challenges for healing when a boy has been sexually abused by a woman.

How and what one believes and feels about women as one develops into and becomes a man will be deeply influenced by this early experience. Healing requires that a man understand and learn to separate himself from any residual toxic models of relationship with women. He needs to find the will and the courage to replace these models in his inner experience with women he can respect, love and trust.

The boy is deeply shamed and confused by the implicit or explicit sense that his body, his privacy and his sexuality belong to and/or are under the control of another person. Whether the abuser is male or female the child's developmental immaturity and lack of experience limit his ability to understand. His maturation is distorted by this intrusion into his natural developmental progression. This early experience with a woman can complicate the adult man's sexuality differently, but no less, than can abuse by a man.

The huge rings around my mother's breasts are often vivid in my visions and dreams of her naked body as she lies seductively on her back while I gaze down on her. But when I was a little boy she took me in her arms and lifted me on top of her and lay back on her bed and hugged me to her. I also remember her kneeling on the floor, with me backed up against her bedside, and sucking my cock. And I have to ask myself if all this kiddie-porn reeling in my brain actually happened. Did she really caress my scrotum and stroke my cock and excite and fluster me? I didn't know whether to accept the pleasure or flee in terror or hang my head in shame. The same ambivalence haunts my adult sexual encounters, and I wonder, How do I get laid without ultimately feeling victimized?

George I

I remember being possibly eight years old and being in the basement with my baby-sitter. I was a very innocent, naive and shy boy. I asked her what she wanted to do. She smiled and knocked me on the cold basement floor and pulled my pants down and began to fondle me. I was taught never to hit girls, so my only defense was to "leave" my body. I used the same defense with my father. By detaching my mind from my body, I was able to survive. This experience and several others made me fear and hate women. This brings another ingredient to the recipe. If I hate women, I must be gay. . . . My mother did nothing to protect me. My mother treated me as a boyfriend and regarded me as a sex object. It was very common for her to whistle at me and sexualize me. I was also given the task of helping her get dressed and undressed. It seems I was the one that had to pick up the slack for my father and help my mother get her various needs met.

John

Confusion and shame haunt the boy: the body responds and the boy enjoys the closeness. At the same time, he knows that something is not right with this experience.

I was abused in my parents' bed, after I came home from primary school. It was the only time my mother let me get close. I would cuddle up to her and she would rub her genitals against mine. I didn't understand what was going on. I would bury my head in the eiderdown to try and block out what was happening. I was ashamed because I enjoyed it. . . . When I read the story of a survivor who was forced to perform oral sex on his mother, I was flooded with emotion. Somehow I knew it had happened to me, starting when I was three. I can still recall the revulsion I used to feel whenever I sat on my mother's lap.

Chris

For Fondling Me

by Jerome

For fondling me furtively, mother dear;
    for fondling me in front of my family
too menaced by your madness to interfere;
    for fondling me in spite of plea after plea
of mother, please, please don't, it makes me feel sick—
    for all those sins, mother, for all those crimes,
with clubs, brass knuckles, axes and arsenic
    I'd kill you in my mind a thousand times.
And yet, in later years, did I not try
    forgiving and forgetting what you had done;
and wasn't I, when came your time to die,
    at bedside weeping same as any son.
We reconciled before it was too late,
and oh, the love I felt, and still the hate.

My mother did little or nothing to stop my father's rages. She would bathe me as a little boy and stand me on the toilet seat to dry me off. That was ok, but she did that until I was twelve. She would even dry off my just beginning to grow pubic hair and run her fingers through it. I was terribly shamed by that.

Roy

How lovely to have your warm little cock in my mouth No harm in that After all you said, Look, my penie is straight At first I was flustered but my little man always looks so scrumptious How soft and clean he is and how small and cuddly lying there on his back giggling with his hand rubbing himself Not like that big hairy bastard with his musty stink always trying to pin me down and stick it in even when I'm tired and dry and I'd even rather vacuum the apartment than land on my back and then end up all sticky between my thighs But you're my little man and so grateful for my attentions and you can't even come to spoil it all. . .

Anyhow I've got you my little man Now that we're through I'll slip my robe back on and pin your diaper up And don't you say anything to your father, Johnny Boy

George I

The boy struggles to tolerate the dissonance of betrayal and trust, injury and affection, violation by the protector, and still go on with his developmental tasks.

DEMISE

by Scott

abused children
abuse
children
when
he was 6
he
had to play
"tickle"
with
neighbor girl
mother
watching
whole time
fingering
herself

CHAPTER 7

THE RANGE OF ABUSE

FROM "IT NEVER GOT BEYOND FONDLING . . ." TO "I HAD BEEN RAPED, TORTURED, TERRORIZED . . ."

The range of abuse is staggering, from the "no big deal" of being fondled by a choirmaster (or a neighbor, or a sister, or a friend) to the unimaginable horror of ritualized abuse.

The range of impact on the boy who suffers the abuse and the man who survives it is likewise broad. There are many variables which determine how the abuse lives in the individual boy, and each boy's experience of abuse is unique, but there is also a direct and proportionate relationship between cause and effect . . . and abuse is abuse.

Healing requires the acknowledgment that the abuse always matters. From its less severe to its most horrific forms, it's always "a big deal." This is a fundamental truth we need to claim for ourselves.

We gain a great deal by choosing to see, eyes wide open, the ways in which what happened to us as boys has shaped our lives as men. Our lives begin to make more sense when we connect the abuse with the ways we operate in the world. Our feelings of paralysis, powerlessness, and feeling frozen or hypnotized during the abuse experience itself; strategies for forgetting, somehow shutting out what was happening; confusion: we begin to see them all in a different light.

It would always start with him pulling my shirt out from my pants, and to this day I panic when someone touches my shirt. It's like he's still here haunting me. . . . It wasn't until I was talking to a counselor who pointed out that any genital stimulation will feel pleasurable even if the situation is not. This was a major source of the guilt I had felt all these years, feeling like a participant, because he could make me get an erection. . .

A few times he asked to keep my underwear so I'd have to go home and quickly get a new pair out of the drawer without my brother noticing and sneak into the bathroom to change. The only way to forget about it was to dive into my homework . . .

Gene

It wasn't so much the sex with Brad that made me feel awful. When I cringe, remembering the sex, it's never because of the act itself. What has always made my stomach clench like a fist is the way Brad's voice and face changed. He became a different person. When we had sex, he seemed to like me.

Eric I

One day, during lunch, we were in the boys' locker room. Frankly, I have no idea why we were there. In retrospect, perhaps it wasn't an accident. We started playing around, per usual, and the quick flurry came. However, my teacher friend missed. One of his blows caught me square in the groin and I doubled over. As he bent down to see if I was all right, my hand shot out and I returned the favor. Delighted with the painful excursion, we started exchanging lower blows and gradually the blows began metamorphosing to caresses. By this time, I had developed an embarrassing reaction in my pants which he noticed and offered to "take care of" for me. He had us take our pants off and I got my first look at his throbbing cock. Ours were the same size. He put my hand on his and he bent down to start kissing me.

He taught me a lot that day. He taught me what the numbers "6" and "9" really meant. He taught me what a man's balls smell like. He taught me how good it feels to have a tongue in your asshole. He taught me to fear other people and hate myself.

Scott

The boy's willingness and ability to trust not only others but also his own perceptions and reactions is a frequent casualty of the abuse experience. As men we need to recognize the severity and significance of effect this early experience as boys continues to have on us today. All forms of abuse carry this residual influence. We need to be able to trust ourselves and others. This is crucial to our healing as adults.

At least once I was sexually abused by a man in a bear suit. We were told it was part of an Indian ceremony. A pipe was passed around for us to smoke, and then the children were passed around, too. The man sat me on his lap and sodomized me, and again I felt nothing, just nothing.

Also at this camp I was deliberately hypnotized. Always in a director's office. I am given very specific instructions not to remember what happened. . . . His words: "Now you don't see anything on the floor, do you; there was no dog, and nothing happened. These people are here to hear you tell them about the camp." And then I cannot see the dog at all. When I come out of the trance, they thank me for telling them about the camp. . . . Another part of me, perception and trust of my perception, was crushed.

A Survivor

Mark felt faint, yet stiff as a board. He could hear Gerry's voice—Gerry was still talking and Mark could hear himself respond. Mark felt as if he had left his body and was watching this pervert hover over him, touching him. No one to Mark's memory, other than his childhood pediatrician, had touched his penis. No girls—he had only kissed a few girls. Now this guy was touching it and Mark couldn't do a thing about it. Mark felt his penis begin to harden. "Oh my God," thought Mark.

For a period of time, Gerry sat there talking, stroking Mark's penis. Gerry never flinched and always smiled, keeping a steady and almost hypnotic voice. He dominated Mark. Mark did not know what they were talking about, and had no concept of time. He did not know what was happening to him. He later only saw Gerry leaving the room, smiling, saying something about breakfast in a few minutes.

Mark

Often, the boy survives by "dissociating," or leaving his body and separating one part of self from the experience of another part of self, during all or part of the abuse experience. The man tends to react in similar ways when "triggered" by stimuli which feel threatening to his emotional capacities.

One of the strangest aspects of these memories is the absence of any image involving his genitals. I remember him nude. I remember his hardness in my mouth, him pushing against my body. But I see no penis. It is as if I went through the whole thing with my eyes closed.

Mike

The tendency to minimize, normalize (after all, "boys will be boys"!), or invalidate the significance of our early experience is a continuing obstacle to our healing as men.

I was twelve when I began piano and voice lessons with my church choirmaster. Under the pretense of feeling my diaphragm, he would put his hands down my pants and start fondling me. Then he would have me do the same to him. This happened every week for three years. It never got beyond fondling, and I never thought it was a big deal.

Chris

CHAPTER 8

A PICTURE'S WORTH A THOUSAND WORDS

CHARLIE'S DRAWINGS

Charlie Wolfe is an artist who lives in the Washington, D.C. area. His work has been featured in solo exhibitions and in a collaborative exhibit of works by survivors presented by Tears of the Children, Inc. titled "A Crying Shame: Images and Stories from the International Collection." In addition to a wide range of other work, Mr. Wolfe has produced over two hundred color-pencil drawings depicting aspects of his childhood experience as a victim of sexual abuse. The drawings reproduced here have been a part of his personal psychotherapy and recovery, and depict a degree of betrayal and trauma which is simply beyond word's ability to tell.

Mr. Wolfe provides us here with powerful windows into the ways childhood sexual abuse infects the very core of the survivor. His drawings speak for themselves.

TODAY MAY '91

BAD
BOY
BAD BOY
BAD BOY
BAD BOY
BAD BOY

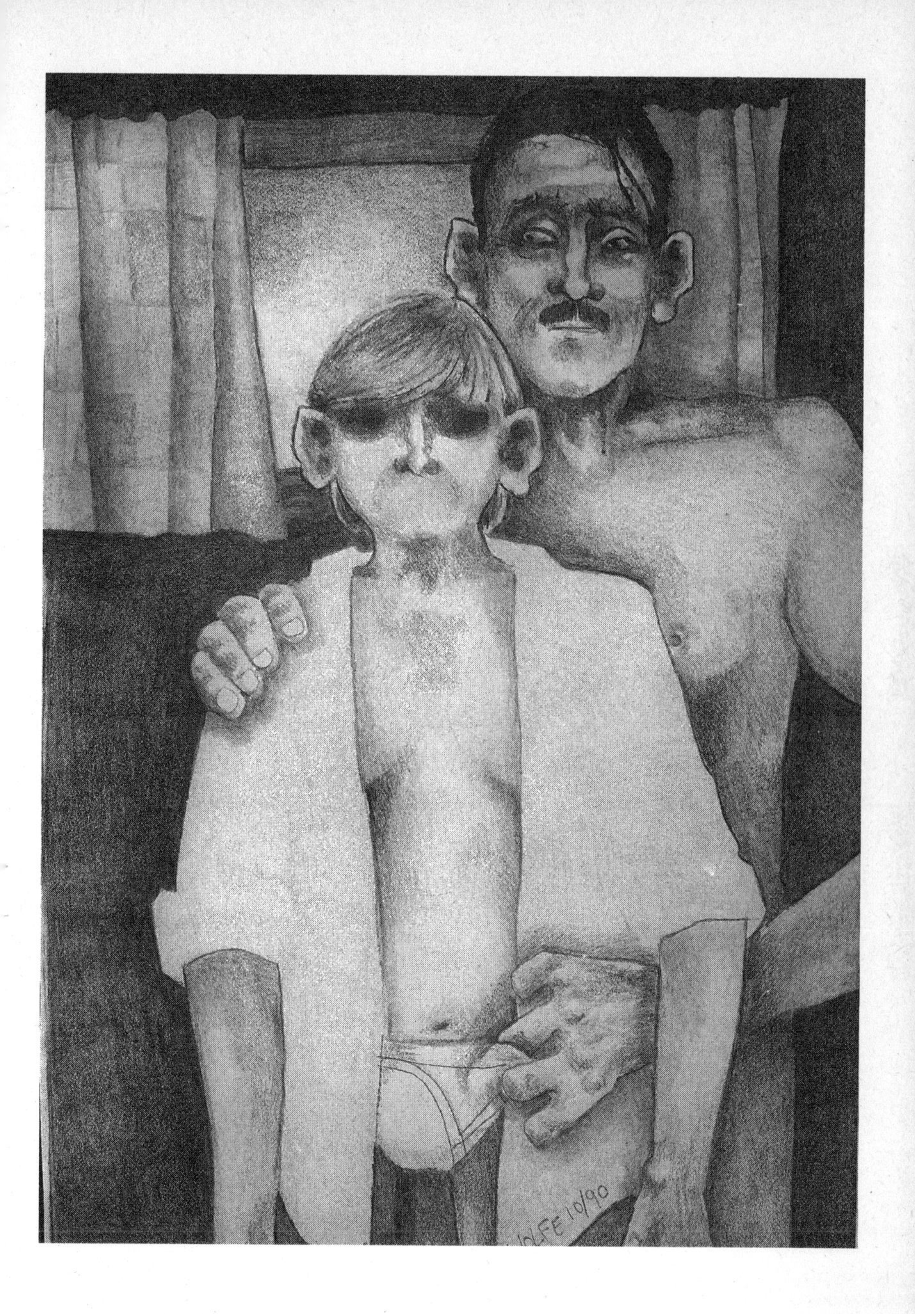

NEVER TaLK
OPEN THaT MOUTH aND
YOU WILL WISH
YOU
NEVER HaD
BEEN
BORN

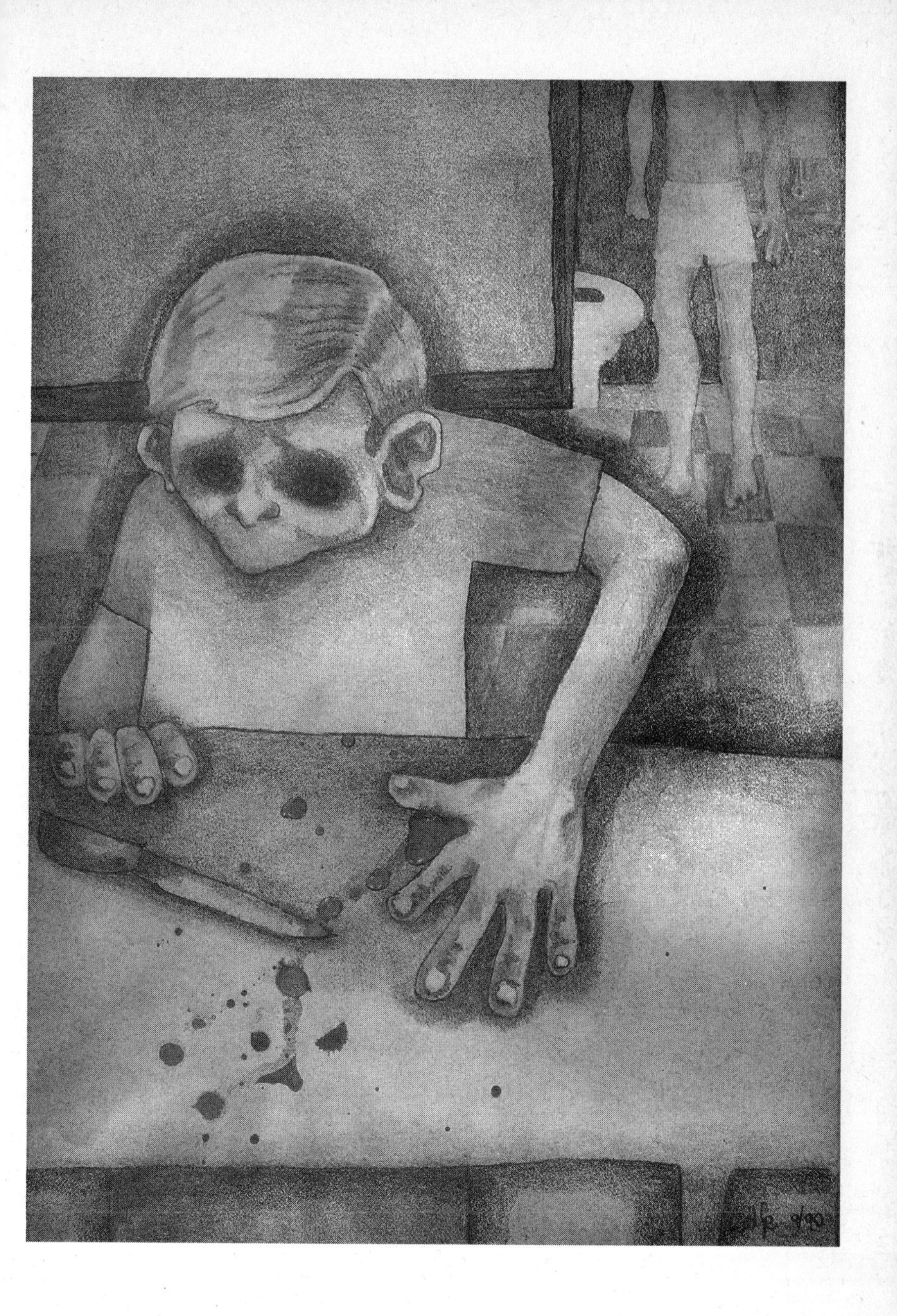

FOREVER LOST

WOLFE

The Children are Upset. They Want TO go HOME,
I can't LET them. I REMEMbER!
6200

PART THREE

FACING THE EFFECTS

Confronting the Long-Held Feelings

CHAPTER 9

SEXUALITY AND INTIMACY

"I HAVE EXPERIENCED A CERTAIN AMOUNT OF SEXUAL CONFUSION"

Once we've faced what's happened to us, we need to get to the task of facing what the effects have been and still are in our lives. As a direct result of childhood sexual abuse, confusion inhabits the survivor's soul on many levels. The related realms of sexuality and intimacy seem to have particular relevance to the male survivor. These realms combine and, for the survivor, confuse issues of trust, vulnerability, power, victimization, learned behavior, sexual orientation, and male identity.

Bringing clarity and healing into these realms is no less than the key to satisfactory adult relationships, with ourselves and with others. This requires facing the enduring effects of the boy's trauma in the man's life.

There comes a point where the confusion has been in charge long enough. We need to take back our lives and take control over the complex effects of the abuse that obstruct our settling into focused, productive, and satisfying relationships, in our private lives and in the larger community.

My abuse has robbed me of full sexual pleasure and the ability to let go of control. . . . I have been sexually abused by men and women. Overtly and covertly. I have clear memories and not such clear memories. The one thing that is completely clear is the effects that are evident in my life today. I have spent many years furious at women and terrified of men. I never knew why. Until now.

John

Post-traumatic stress is what I call my condition. The addictions were just deadly symptoms of childhood assault and abuse. Every relationship I have is or was affected by this trauma to some degree. My parents were not involved in the rape. Mental and physical abuse and torture were more their style. This left me with a rip in my protective aura as a child. Kind of like a kick-me sign—only worse.

C.L.

I have memories of my father masturbating me when I was an infant. He was never violent with me. Violence was a sin, as was sodomy. But he rationalized and did everything else. I grew up with no sense of boundaries. I was basically at my father's disposal, until I was ten or eleven. I don't believe that the abuse happened often, only when dad had the opportunity. There was fondling of my genitals and body. I had his penis in my mouth and he kissed me all over my body, especially my mouth and genitals. I became aroused by this, and my sexuality was permanently warped.

Murray

These were largely lost, often dark years, of bohemianism and experimentation with drugs and varieties of sexual experience, of holding on to and letting go of a variety of partners and jobs, of living on the margins of society and, later, of compulsive buying and spending, of workaholism, of a deafening deadness of spirit. They were years of running from myself and the pursuing cacophony within.

Neal

Often the perpetrator will actively seek to blame the boy for the abuse, to make the victim feel like the responsible party. The boy is blamed for the abuse with the implication that he somehow wanted or caused it to happen.

Sexist and homophobic messages from the larger culture are often attached to the attempt to blame the boy for the abuse and complicate his efforts to understand his experience. This can greatly distort the boy's developing gender and sexual identities. His overall understanding of sex and sexuality, including sexual orientation and the relation of sex to affection and vulnerability are affected.

This can deeply complicate our eventual development as men who are joyfully both sexual and loving.

They told me "That's what girls do. That's what your mom does to your dad. If you tell anybody, they'll all think you're like a girl. You won't have any girlfriends, you suck boys." These weren't the exact words, but the messages were planted deeply within me. Somehow, I was bad. I was odd. I was inferior. I was not desirable because of what I had done.

Joe

Oddly enough, I had never suppressed or forgotten these memories; I remembered them like a bad movie I had seen long ago. I had even mistakenly romanticized my experiences into the fantasy of father-son sex prevalent in certain gay male circles. It was only after many years of recovery in Alcoholics Anonymous that I realized that being gay was not a source of my problems. It was only when my emotions began to unfreeze that I realized they had been frozen, since the age of five. . . .

From what I have heard in the rooms of incest recovery, I have come to believe that male children perceived as incipient homosexuals are prone to being sexually abused by adults, much the way female children are vulnerable to such abuse.

Les

All my sexual desire for other women gets mixed up in my erotic relationship with my mother. It's a love-hate feeling toward her and them, all of them eventually seeming to be bitches like her. It's a wonder I'm not gay for all the bile I sometimes feel toward women.

George I

The heterosexual man, whose perpetrator was a man, wonders if the abuse can make him gay (it doesn't and can't) or happens to him because he really is gay (unlikely, if he's straight he's straight). The gay or bisexual man wonders if he's gay or bisexual because he's been abused (definitely not, enduring myths notwithstanding). And all of us, regardless of sexual orientation, can easily confuse residual effects of the abuse with what would have otherwise been our "natural" sexuality. This complicates arriving at certainty about our orientation, sexual desires, and ability to form quality intimate relationships.

"How could you let that guy do that?," thought Mark to himself. "How could you get a hard-on from a guy! What the fuck is the matter with you?! Are you a queer?!"

Mark

Even though kids on the schoolyard called each other *gay* and *fag*, I wasn't sure what it meant. When I found out, I was horrified that I was one and didn't even know it. I now had another reason to keep this ugly secret to myself, because I was afraid of the unspeakable, [which to] a seventh grader [was that] people would think you were gay. As if adolescence isn't confusing enough, right about this time I started noticing all the girls developing breasts and was mesmerized by them. That's when the abuse took on the homosexual perspective, but it had been going on for so long and I didn't know what to do. This does, however, answer the nature versus nurture question regarding homosexuality, in my mind. I was certainly nurtured to respond one way, but was early on and remain an avowed "boob man."

Gene

It's essential to recognize that sexual orientation and sexual confusion are very different from one another. For the male survivor, it often takes time to sort out what one's true orientation is and what instead is learned behavior, the imprinted "arousal pattern" learned from the abuse experience. Regardless of our adult orientation, the part of a man's sexuality imprinted by the abuse has nothing to do with his true sexual nature; if he hadn't been abused as a boy, his sexuality would almost certainly not include this aspect.

I honestly haven't had that many [cocks]. In fact, I'm married and I don't really consider myself gay. I haven't had sex with a man in over two years. Not that I've ever enjoyed it. My resolve simply seems to turn to quivering mush when confronted with masculine lust. I don't get excited so much as . . . nervous. It's like feeling as though I'm going to get a failing grade on a final, only worse.

Scott

I have experienced a certain amount of sexual confusion. I know I am heterosexual, but there have been many times in my life when I have experienced certain attractions to men and children, which make no sense. . . . I have grown up with compulsions around sex. Sex has been quite separate from love and affection for me. I masturbate almost every day. I have been strongly attracted to "kinky" sex, without knowing why. I tend to be very passive in sexual situations, which further destroys any chance of developing a healthy relationship.

Murray

I continued my compartmentalized life; I participated more deeply in gay sex, moving into sadomasochistic and ritualized sex activities, while at the same time struggling to create and develop meaningful emotional and sexual relationships with a succession of lovely young women. In my professional compartment, I rose through the ranks quickly, earned two additional professional degrees from a prestigious university in record time, taught part time at two other universities, and established a "moonlight" architectural practice. I started a classic psychoanalytic therapy process, seeing my therapist five sessions a week.

Eric III

The boy's confusion makes perfect sense. Children and adolescents coerced or manipulated into sexual activity before they are emotionally, psychologically, and physically ready to consent to mutual sexual activity are bound to wind up with profoundly befuddled beliefs and feelings about sexual behavior and intimate relationships.

"Do you want to suck it?," Brad asks. He straddles my head as he sits on the table. I take his penis into my mouth. At first he does not touch me. But then he grabs the back of my head and forces his penis roughly into my mouth. He ejaculates quickly, silently. The whole process lasts less than two minutes.

As soon as he's done he stands up, turning away from me. He pulls his pants back up. The Scrabble game lies unfinished in a shadow. The water heater blows on. I try to talk with him.

"Let's finish the game."

"No."

"But I thought you wanted to play."

Silence. He is doing up his belt.

"I was winning," I say.

"I was letting you win," Brad says, "you little faggot."

He turns to go into his room, and slams the door. I sit there in silence. I hear Brad's stereo go on. After a while I hear Mother upstairs with my sisters, and then Dad comes home from work. I sit at the table downstairs for a long time. I feel sick to my stomach, sick at heart. It's happened before. It will probably happen again. The whole thing is somehow my fault. Brad never comes out of his room.

Eric I

I remember being ten or eleven and having a school friend tell me "all about" sex. He told me that my parents "fucked," that was how babies were born. I remember being really afraid that I might be pregnant, that somehow everyone would discover me and that I couldn't be a boy anymore. I went through a real panic attack over this.

Mike

The childhood abuse caused a lot of confusion in my sexuality. I enjoy having sex with a woman—it's deeply satisfying, physically and emotionally—and yet, I did have sex for years with a man (although I thought of him as my father) some of which was also physically enjoyable and, to some degree, emotionally rewarding.

Guy

Sorting out what is truly his own natural sexuality and what has been imprinted by the abuse is equally hard work for the gay, straight, or bisexual man. It's hard work; it's important work.

My first experience was as a boy of twelve in Los Angeles, California. Although the experience is defined as molestation because of the age difference, I found the experience to be quite pleasurable and became an active and agreeable participant. My molester was my sixteen-year-old female cousin who was living with us at the time.

My other experience which was molestation and more came in Tucson when I was thirteen. . . . Afterwards he cleaned me up and showed me his erect penis and thanked me for helping him get an erection. He gave me a dime and drove me back to the grocery store. I never told anyone. I must admit that his causing me to come was a new experience. I had never masturbated before but after this experience I began masturbating at least once a day. I also got my half-sister to masturbate me while I fingered her.

Before these experiences I had never given much thought to the pleasurable feelings associated with sexual activities. However, because of these experiences I began numerous fantasies, usually with a young, inexperienced girl. In my fantasies, the girls were always willing participants who enjoyed the experience.

George II

Several years later, when he would spend hours slowly reaching his own hand into a friend's sleeping bag or across the bedcovers to touch and fondle them, he would feel the same fear and fascination until he returned the covers to their gentle caress of the male body. He would be mesmerized and would freeze in fear if they rolled over or made snoring noises. He didn't remember the Bogeyman during those times though. He just felt like some kind of monster.

Jimmy

It's very challenging for the male survivor to seek his personal truth about sexuality and intimacy in a culture that is itself confused about gender roles, sexuality, and sexual orientation. Sadly, ours is a culture which continues to perpetuate a great deal of ignorance and harmful mythology in these areas.

While we know that sexual abuse does not and cannot cause sexual orientation, and makes a man no less a man for having been abused, we also know that sexual abuse almost always does cause sexual confusion.

Most fundamentally this confusion is about trust and touch and sex as a loving expression between two equal partners, rather than as an exploitative manipulation that is "done to" one.

The resolution of this confusion results in nothing less than the full, rich, and mature relating of one adult with another.

CHAPTER 10

RAGE

"YOU FILTHY BASTARD"

Any depth of recovery has to involve the many levels of feeling we have inside at what was done to us as children. For most of us, this eventually involves the surfacing of rage. This is natural, important, and appropriate. It's enormously painful to feel what's been taken from us as boys by our perpetrators, and to see the many ways this theft has molded our developmental experience as adolescents and adults.

Because the child frequently blames, and often comes to hate, himself as a result of the abuse, it's essential to get clear about who's responsible for what happened. Whether we confront our perpetrator(s) in person (never essential) or indirectly through a letter not sent, in therapy, or some other means, doesn't really matter. Many of us will never experience forgiveness of our perpetrators, nor do we have to in order to heal. What we do have to do as men is allow ourselves to feel the full range of reaction to what was done to us as boys.

The boy is never the responsible party, and he has every right to be angry, very angry.

Sadly, we often blame the wrong person. What should be rage at whoever did this to us is experienced instead as rage and hatred at ourselves for "letting it happen." This feeling can particularly plague older boys, who are no less innocent of responsibility for the abuse than younger boys, but who feel they should have been able to prevent it from happening.

The next morning, Mark was up before the dawn's light. He felt a tightness overwhelming his entire body. He took a long hot shower. He felt dirty. He let it happen to himself again. He needed someone to help him. He hated himself.

Mark

It takes so much youthful energy, which is then not available for simply being a boy (our real *job at that stage of life), to bottle up all our rightful rage and indignation.*

I remember two things about him that particularly repelled me: his smell and his hairiness. I hated touching him; I hated putting my mouth on him. I always gagged. And I hated his cum. I didn't know what cum was. To me, it was urine. I was something he pissed on.

Mike

My reflection floated in his blue eyes. For a moment, I saw myself falling into them and disappearing. I almost wanted that to happen, to be swallowed up, to be held and protected and preserved by another person's body. To have somebody else do it all for me, all the thinking, the living.

Robert

I was nineteen before I refused to have sex with you . . . and yet I felt rejected by you, so intense was your emotional control. It only ended at age twenty-one because I was able to physically get away into the navy.

Guy

I never knew for sure whether I was gay, bi, or heterosexual, or just damned with a sexual instinct I could never control or satisfy. I could consciously remember since about age five a sexual attraction for other boys that looked like you—only that had blond hair. This haunted me for a lifetime until I realized I was only reacting to fear of boys who looked similar to you and had the fear confused with sexual attraction.

Jim

I remember being fourteen and home alone with him. I'm sure he had not touched me in three or four years. He thought he was having a heart attack and called out for help. I went into the living room and watched him thrash in pain. I stood watching, hoping he would die, letting him die without rescue. He knew. I felt cold-blooded. I have no remorse. . . .

I received a Christmas card from him today. I am numbed by his audacity.

Mike

On the outside I presented an image of contentment, acceptance, compliance, and inner peace. I remember how keenly I felt the gripping power of my rage toward the abuser, who was well-known and esteemed by the order. I kept creating angry speeches, vengeful reproaches and hateful soliloquies in my inner self. I was often involved in periods of inner debate with myself, my classmates, the studentmaster, the superior of the house, my parents, and, yes, even God.

Louis

I was only three when you took advantage of me as the innocent child I was and used me as a damn masturbation object for your own selfish pleasure that may have lasted only a few minutes and gave you a few seconds of ecstasy. You filthy bastard fucked up the first and best forty years of my life with that act. . . . All that I realized thirty-seven years later is what I saw, what I physically felt, and a couple of words you said to me after you got your damned nut off. The lasting effects that devastated my love, trust, and sexual relationships, my life, for the years that followed were a nightmarish confusion about my own fear, anger, and sexual instincts and constant inner turmoil and conflicts that my mind and body were telling me. I ended up hating myself and life itself instead of you and what you did to me. . . . You had fucked me out of a normal growing up as a youth, adolescent, and adult. My relationships with people and personal intimate relationships with girlfriends had been completely fucked up and I was never able to learn or experience what natural love, sexual attraction, and relationships were all about. Fear and shame of all that had emotionally crippled and paralyzed me all my life. I had everything else going for me that seemed important in life, but all of that became so unimportant to me without being able to have love and relationships in my life that are a natural and human need.

Jim

THE POEM I'VE SPENT MY LIFE TRYING NOT TO WRITE

by C.A.

when I saw the old man again
I shook the hand that tickled my balls at five
that sent my small stiff cock shivering
past the slick gums and cheeks
the hand that worked my small hairless body into a blackout
and woke me up
with a slap
to open my fresh peach-can mouth
for his smelly dirty old prick and I cried
he liked it when I cried

I shook the hand that shoved two
or was it three fingers up my ass
until I shit in his palm
until I ripped and started bleeding
and the sight of a torn tomato still sends me to tears
still shows me the difference I am
still makes me walk with a limp

but I shook the hand
I knelt before the hand and kissed it

he said boy what are you doing?

I said I'm paying homage to the hand that stopped my clock
the hand that took me out of one world
and punctured me screaming through the skin of another

a world where my mother grew bigger and meaner
and never allowed honesty again
a world where God grew smaller and smaller
and disappeared one day

I kissed the hand and laid it over my heart
but the hand did not know how it destroyed
and slid under my belt
and my cock stiffened in its grip

O my the old man said you really have grown
you've really flowered and I'd sure like you up my ass he said
I've got a fresh jar of KY jelly
can you give this old bird another taste?

I kissed him once and bent him over where he couldn't see me
greasing my daddy's 12 gauge I had hidden in the corner
and I shoved it up his hairy old
pink old smelly old asshole
'cause man I'm going BACK
I'm riding the black storm back
to the world I BELONG
where my mother still believed in me
where a boy can play in a sandbox
and dream
and still say no
to old men waving Dairy Queen hot fudge sundaes

and save his own life at five
and never have to burn like an ant
beneath the magnifying glass of God and scrutiny
and you won't have to walk home so funny
so different

I want that boy to be a brave little man
and I shove my daddy's 12 gauge
clear up this old fucker's shithole
and let the motherfucker BLOW
just like my daddy would've done
if my daddy had loved me enough
to let him know

The rage can make surprise appearances in our current lives, despite our best efforts to banish it once and for all. That's okay. As long as we've gotten to know it for what it is, even befriended it as well as we can, the rage can't hurt us or others.

A good man leans his weight upon my back, breathes in my ear, wraps his arm in affection high on my chest, near my neck. He means well, and whispers words of healing neither he nor I had ever heard said to us. "I'm glad you're here, son. I'm glad you're a boy."

His arm is too tight across my throat. His raspy breath is eerily familiar. I feel a cold splash of memory returning, like the first leaks in a crumbling dike presage the loosing of pent-up waters.

I break the circle of men and leave the gathering to stand alone in a dandelion meadow high up under the rain shadow of the Olympian Mountains. I pry my fingers from the holes in the patchwork barrier I built when I was seven. I built well. I contained this sewage for thirty-four years.

Memory floods and overwhelms me, rushing me back to a bedroom of a tenement on the South Side of Chicago.

This time, my vantage point is not perched safely in a corner, watching a boy who looks like me being raped. I am in my body. My father's arm is tight across my throat, arching my back. He is exhaling hard, in rhythm, as he shows me why he is glad I am his son.

Twenty years since I found his body, dead by his own hand.

I rage that he is not alive today, so I could strangle him with my own hands.

I hunger for a dish of vengeance, a repast of revenge. Cold around the edges. Hot as molten lead at the core.

Scott Abraham

RAGE

by Brett

Rage, how do I miss thee?
With passion and tremor
Delirium and effortful inspiration
Lost yet sought
And
Feared, yet vital.

Rage, how do I transform thee?
Into brilliance, light and ease
To be known and praised,
Loved and held,
yet flailing and hurting.

Rage, how do I occupy thee?
Frightful apparition of death within my inner mind
Or natural essence of healing—
Generation and confusion.

Rage, how do I hold thee?
To do me no damage and
Spare me your evil rod of memories
Which bore you into my world
And from which I cannot erase you.

Rage, now how do I say thee?
Precious and frightening on a grand scale

And newly loved, but despised
Yet more feared
The words escape me yet.

Rage, how do I follow thee?
In great need and pleasant turmoil
Upon the surface of my days
You are the clement
For me you are a delight.

Rage, you have lost me
In whirlwinds of delight
And fright
And pain and sorrow
But rage,
You are past, and present,
I am only present,
for which I love you, and me,
Rage, on this paper,
I adore thee.

I hate what the abuse has done to me. I don't deserve to have to squander my life's resources and energies on living through the aftershocks. No one has the right to hurt another human being to this degree—devastation. My abusers have a lot to atone for.

Guy

An exercise in the workshop had us pretend that the other person we were addressing was someone who had hurt us (possibly, but not necessarily, our perpetrator). We were asked to respond to two questions. How have I hurt you? and, What can I do to help you?

The answers that passed through my lips surprised me. I had been quite certain that I would be unable to react to such direct questions, especially coming from a complete stranger. The driving feeling that surfaced was one of not wanting my perpetrator to help me in any way—even if he could. Allowing him to do so might help him absolve himself of what he had done to me. That is something I would never want him to feel. Small traces of anger came through as well, in terms of wanting him to feel the same kind of pain that I'd been made to feel.

More than anything else, I wanted him to leave me alone. He still won't leave me alone . . . even after all these years . . . even though he's dead now. . . .

Nick

You are ready for your life to stop stagnating. You are ready to walk, even run in the opposite direction. You wish for him to sit in this chair, as you have for twenty years: in his pain like excrement and let it permeate him—become him—let him be the shit you have been made to feel you were. . . . May there be so much of it that he will be unable to move for twenty years or more.

S.K. Duff

Often others who love us show us in their own reactions how enormously angry we deserve to be at what happened to us. This challenges all we've come to accept about it being our fault, and not deserving either compassion or love, from ourselves or another.

She's really been the hero through all this. I was so surprised that she got so upset and angry. She was beside herself for weeks unable to control her emotions. She wanted to control her emotions. She wanted to kill him. She was mad at me for not telling her, not trusting that she'd understand. She was mad at my family for not protecting me. She was mad at the whole situation and there was nothing she could do to change it. I wasn't ready for the barrage of reaction that I got, all the while I was moved that she loved me so much. The best "high" from this experience is the greater depth in our relationship that I didn't think was possible.

Gene

For a long time I hated myself. I accepted myself as the modern day anti-Christ, the ultimate villain. Of all the marks my abuser branded me with, this might be his last and greatest. He has made me a bit of him. That has started to pass and I'm beginning to understand myself as neither hero nor villain but survivor.

David I

PART FOUR

THE HOME STRETCH: TAKING CONTROL

Recovery, Integration, and Moving On

CHAPTER 11

THE HEALING SPIRIT

"I SOUGHT TO MAKE MYSELF WHOLE"

We attempt to contain the effects of our abuse in many different ways. Healing requires that we learn as much as we can about the hidden ways the abuse has become accustomed to living inside us and take away its various and assorted powers in our lives. Then we become the holders of the power.

We gradually reverse the power imbalance we've lived with for so long. The key word here is gradually, for generally speaking the abuse has permeated so many levels and layers and dimensions of our being that we're wise never to become complacent about its residual presence.

Increasingly, with honesty, determination, loving support, and stubbornly resilient spirits we, and not the abuse, are in charge.

We try to hide the reality from ourselves and others. We repeat and imitate what was done to us as an attempt to master it. Fantasy and compulsive behaviors can be frequent attempts at escape for the survivor. They feel private, under our control, ever at our beck and call, comrade and solace in our isolation. They feel safe, but keep us isolated with the abuse as it lives inside of us.

Later I will recognize and recapture this feeling, over and over again with other men. In each sexual encounter with my father I will feel an exquisite terror. I will tremble with fear and desire, I will be consumed by a fascination that both repulses and fascinates me. I will come to believe, in my heart of hearts, that all men secretly desire all men, that all men secretly have sex with each other, that all people, men and women, say one thing while meaning something quite different. And I will discover myself a complete naïf because I will never be able to figure out what the real secret is, what the actual game being played is all about. Life will mystify, terrify, and hold me hostage.

I remember always feeling different, disconnected from other children, constantly felt I was being judged by others, and adversely. I knew somehow I was a "mistake." My sister sent me a videotape she had made a couple of years ago from old home movies from the 1950s and 1960s. I was astounded to see myself appearing and behaving every bit as strange and alien as I had felt growing up. I could see that by the age of ten I was already living in that emotional black hole that I have only recently climbed out of. My life had been unmitigated pain, and I had always thought it was somehow my fault.

I escaped into fantasy—I had many penpals around the world; I had a very active sex life with any male I could seduce. I was also miserable, I felt completely alone, I hated myself, I had only one friend (who was both best friend and primary sexual partner), I retreated into books, TV, and days alone wandering through the forested hills surrounding the valley we lived in.

I learned to utterly mistrust my own instincts, to disbelieve even what was obviously true. I was very gullible, unable to trust. And yet, I had an unwavering knack for choosing to mistrust those in whom I could best rely and to trust those who would assuredly betray and violate me. I had no power over my own body; I could not even control it myself.

Over the years this grew into a full-fledged victim mentality. I was a perfectionist who could never do it right. I was chronically depressed and could never stay emotionally balanced. My thinking grew obsessive, peaking finally in the wake of my ex-lover's abandoning me. I lived with suicidal thinking from my teen years on, having attempted it on several occasions, and free of it only since coming into incest recovery.

I became a full-blown alcoholic and drug addict, in part to escape those awful feelings, in part to capture positive feelings, to appear self-confident and gregarious, to break out of my isolation. I sought to make myself whole through chemical addictions and relationship addictions. I was a workaholic, sex addict, compulsive overeater, excessively fearful. My thought patterns became bogged down in negative thinking, I could not escape my depression. I developed a freeway phobia and would have panic attacks if I drove in the left lanes of high-speed freeway traffic. I stopped driving.

Les

In the years since the active abuse stopped, there have been times when I have unconsciously sought to replicate that sensation in anonymous, random sex—not an affair, just a quick five minutes and run—feeling guilty and unsatisfied.

Guy

I feel like guarding my notebook with my left hand, the way you do in grade school when you're taking a test next to someone who didn't study.

But now it's so my lover can't see what I'm writing. I'm not sure that I ever want him to read this, let alone anyone else. But this is not new to me. Living a life rooted in terror makes hiding seem natural.

A Survivor

A POEM THAT I'VE BEEN THINKING ABOUT FOR A WHILE

by David I

He was nine.
I was twenty-six.

I was seven.
He was older.

I remember his thick strong hand
reaching out towards me.

I remember his soft clean stomach
leading down to his naked pubic skin
and his slender erect penis.

I remember being drawn to him
feeling trust
feeling attention
feeling closed in comfort.

I remember moving magnetic
down and across his body.

I felt small.
I forgot my size and strength.
I got lost.
We were in the basement of his house,

of my girlfriend's house,
of the girl I used to play with's house.

We were in an island cottage,
on a dark summer night.

It was comforting.
I don't remember his body
but now I fear a man's cock
especially when they're large.

I still wanted to be the caring one
even after I had become the wound.

I remember being drawn to him
for the tenderness my parents couldn't give.
I feel it's all a lie now,
but when I remember,
I start to cry.

I grew up feeling like an observer of a mean, senseless society, not being able or allowed to ever fully participate. I had few friends, no girlfriends, and little happiness through high school. I thought that the male role in society was stupid and abusive and cruel. I thought that since I didn't fit the mold, I was not attractive to females and this seemed to be true.

Joe

I'd like to think [the abuse] isn't true. My friends, colleagues, my lover, and my therapists probably don't believe it's true. But, as I learn more about the forty years that make up my face . . . I'm thinking maybe it is true. Because, hard as [it is] for me to believe, the kinds of abuse I endured are so grotesque and debasing, I feel I've been irrevocably altered inside my mind and heart, and though some things are and have been healing, inside I remain disfigured.

A Survivor

The abuse has tentacles which reach into the very heart of the boy's developing sense of self, affecting and interfering in varied ways with how he comes to know and feel about himself.

From the ages of five to forty-three I never attributed anything to the sexual abuse of my youth. I never connected any of the madness in my life to the insanity of the earliest years. I had to suffer an attack on my life before I could hear a small loving voice saying, ". . . it sounds like you were sexually abused as a child."

Well, I knew that. I knew a lot of things, cognitively. But I didn't know I was the victim and not the cause.

Secrets and kisses, our special understanding; my only affection.

David II

My wife . . . was the hardest person to tell. Even after being in a relationship for over fourteen years with her, I was convinced she'd run from the house screaming if she ever knew the real me. She often complained that she only got 90 percent of me and that she couldn't get to that last part. I always knew she was right, though I denied it, but nobody was going to find out about that small percentage. I felt like damaged property and she'd have every right to say I'd deceived her so she would want out. I felt that way about myself.

Gene

I worked at dangerous occupations. I wasn't really aware of trying to compensate for my damaged manhood. Like most men, I was only vaguely aware of the gender conditioning messages society sends to men. It doesn't seem to matter that you were a child when you were sexually assaulted. Men are supposed to defend or die trying. No matter how hard I tried, I never felt I was as good a man as the next: logger, construction worker, or bouncer.

C.L.

SUNDAY SCHOOL TEACHER

by Danny

Home, drunk again.
He must have quit drinking a million
Times over the years.
It wasn't his parents who tried their
Best, nor the women who loved
Him as long as they could, or
His children who don't need to
See him this way.

Maybe it was the Sunday School
Teacher years ago at the local Baptist church
that liked our young innocent golden rods
As he molested us one by one, secretly.
I hear he's doing time now!
So am I, trying to glue the leftover
pieces of my life together one drink
    At a time.

Even when the body's response signals pleasure, the spirit registers the boy's injury and pain.

Mark could not believe what had just happened to him. He was confused, lost, and scared. He was so ignorant of the outside world; among the many thoughts tearing through his mind were: "Do all guys do this?," "Am I supposed to just think nothing of this?," and "Gerry's so much older—he must know what he's doing."

But most of all, Mark felt like he'd been hurt. And that feeling grew by the minute. He hurt from inside. He began to blame himself. . . . Mark wasn't talking, he was sitting in a Greyhound bus seat, but he could feel his chest heaving and his pulse racing. . . . Mark was beginning to not like himself very much. He felt dirty.

Mark

Perhaps the hardest part of this story is not the actual history of what happened to me. Rather, it is the effects of the abuse. . . . When I look at my life now, I don't know where to begin. I think of my nearly complete lack of self-esteem. I think of my inability to form intimate relationships with women. I am generally very awkward around the women I am attracted to. I think this is the result of the tremendous shame I feel about being sexually aroused. I also respond to sexual arousal as a seven year old would. My ex-girlfriend used to complain that I could never be an adult in bed, and she had a point. I have been very isolated and alone for most of my life. Expressing affection for people has generally been difficult for me. I have lived mostly in my brain, cut off from the rest of my experience.

Murray

Sometimes our actions render us horrified that somehow we have become the abuser. The fear of repeating a learned behavior lives, at some point, in every survivor. As a man's past and present become more conscious and available to him, he senses the fine line between feeling and acting. The confusion is profound and may have clouded his judgment in the past.

The abuse of another is never okay; the urge to reverse roles and repeat the experience can be quite strong. The survivor who "fesses up" to himself and others, and who feels his and others' integrity as equally sacred, is the healing victim who is least likely to abuse another.

The moment of my greatest horror came many years after the abuse itself. I one day realized that not only had it been done to me, but I had done it too. *And I didn't even know it!* I had manipulated and exploited others, applying what I had learned as a child. For years, I didn't realize that this wasn't "normal"; I thought this was how people connected sexually. Today, I'm kind of asexual; confused and in constant pain about it all. I have incredible depths of guilt, regret, remorse, and shame in my soul for what I've done to others; it wipes out any compassion for myself and my own abuse. I wish there was some way I could apologize and make it all go away. Maybe just saying this will help somehow. I hope so.

A Survivor

The final trigger to seek help came as our very close friends neared delivery of their first child, and my wife and I discussed having a child of our own. I was deathly afraid I would repeat the cycle of abuse, and I wasn't going to be able to avoid being around their new baby—or perhaps our own, as I had done with other children in the past.

Guy

Safety in self is primary in what our perpetrators have sought to take from us. We need to find and claim this back for ourselves.

As I sit on the shore of the Atlantic on the sands of Cape Cod's beaches, my main thought is that my perpetrator is across the ocean and that I am still scared.

Neither the fact that I haven't seen him in twenty-three years, nor that he has been dead for seven years are enough to make me feel safe. I'm not sure if I'll ever feel safe. . . .

Nick

I experienced dozens of spurting cocks before I ever had my first glimpse of female genitalia. I never once initiated action, but there seemed to be something that drew pedophiles to me. I guess by that age, I might not have been thought of as a child, but men twice my age thought nothing of shoving themselves into my mouth. The final straw was when my doctor begged me to let him stick it up my ass. I felt like I finally understood some of my female friends who have been raped as I frantically sucked him off, hoping he would come and be satisfied. Frankly, I'm not a wimp. In fact I have a very violent streak. I'm not really sure why I have never had the backbone to deal more effectively with these situations. At least I feel relieved in knowing that I haven't had dreams of hell or spurting cocks in years.

Scott

CHAPTER 12

BEGINNING RECOVERY

THE SAFETY OF VULNERABILITY

At some point we find ourselves responding more and more to the insistent urgings of our spirits and our souls, and less and less to the accustomed residue of the abuse. Spirit and soul are tired of being estranged. They long to be rejoined, to finally experience, and celebrate, their natural union.

By now, we've told the secrets, recognized and validated what happened to us, and assigned the responsibility where it belongs. We've seen the effects on our lives today and begun to integrate our long-submerged feelings about our experiences as boys. From here, we feel the increased momentum toward ever greater healing and liberation from the past.

We still have a lot of work to do, and it is a long and gradual process—but we're well on our way.

We can find some humor mixed with our determination. We begin to dig out from under the internal rubble; we start to put the pieces together, moving toward the whole man we've not yet been able to be. We become humbled by what we've accomplished so far, and know that healing has many layers and many levels. Sometimes we even feel like we've already gotten a particular part under control, only to learn that there's more to be done.

It can at times be discouraging, but there's no going back; the spiral is an upward one. Little by little, the abuse has less power over us and we have more power over it.

Next week, after waiting a year, I'm joining our city's first therapy group for male survivors. When I went for an interview, the therapist seemed doubtful. I seemed to have done so much recovery work already. But then he said to me that none of the abuse was my fault, and I burst into tears. I've come a long way, but I've got a long, long way to go.

Chris

I joke that I would rather have open-heart surgery without anesthesia, than deal with these issues.

It reminds me of when I was a child and would stall to do my homework. I would set homework time aside and suddenly realize that my room needed to be cleaned, or I needed to finish a project, paint something (anything), or just stare into space. I would do virtually anything to avoid thinking, feeling, uncomfortability, responsibility, fear, or pain. I have definitely carried that trait into my present-day life. I refuse to let the grass grow under my feet. I learned a long time ago that feelings can't hit a moving target.

John

I lay very still, wondering how to make my fear real to Mandy. Wondering if I knew him well enough to even talk about it or even if I could talk about it. These thoughts paralyzed me. All I wanted to do was leave and start over again tomorrow. It struck me then that this happened with everyone I got close to. . . . Something gripped me, twisting my body and my thoughts into something I could hide behind, a shield of perfect armor, an animal better protected against love and feeling than an armadillo or a porcupine.

The rest of my dream became words and then I told him that a long time ago that happened to me. I told him that when I'm awake, I can't even remember half of it. That sometimes I wonder if it even happened. "Sometimes I go so long, I can almost convince myself it never happened," I said. Then I told him that I had never said any of those things to anyone before, not even my mother.

"I want to make it go away for you," Mandy said.

"You can't," I answered. "I've tried for years."

"Stop trying and let somebody else do it for awhile."

He pulled me close and his hands felt strong. I thought, just for a moment, that hands that strong just might be able to make it go away. But then I knew. It was inside of me and all I could do was try to understand it.

Robert

There's no one road to recovery and healing. Travel on any road takes great courage. We each need to start out on the road that's right for us.

The fact that I became a drug addict tells me that I stayed frozen in terror and shame for almost twenty years. I have heard it said in recovery meetings, as I am now over seven years clean and sober, that the booze and dope saved our lives. At least until we could find real help. I wonder how many of us survivors there are who found the numbing escape of dope and booze the only reason we did not eat a bullet rather than face the shame. Because of this male closeting, I feel the actual statistics on make survivors is quite misleading at present. Maybe as more men find the courage to confront the myths and throw off the conditioning, then also, more men will seek the safety of vulnerability.

C.L.

And then it happened. My catharsis came; and much to my embarrassment, as a Barbra Streisand movie . . . in *The Prince of Tides,* when the child Nick Nolte character is being raped, my stomach hurt (once again) to the point of puking. . . . I rushed to the bathroom and upon leaving the theater I rushed to the baths, now seeking sex as an escape—no longer as the clues to my remembering.

S.K. Duff

Allowing the man's grief for what the boy lost to his abuse, and for the burden the man has since carried, is an extremely important part of healing. This grief can be enormous and consuming; the boy couldn't afford to feel it. The man must.

In the last two years I have come to understand how the multiple incestings and other abuse I experienced as a child traumatized me, shamed me into grievously false beliefs about myself, and set me up to sabotage my own life. My life had become like a movie in which I was a victim of the universe and powerless over anything. I spent years describing this feeling as a kind of "emotional AIDS"—I was vulnerable to anything and everyone that crossed my path. I had no emotional boundaries, but the incesting had so disabused me of any sense of personal autonomy over my body, my perceptions, or my soul that I was not capable of realizing I hadn't any boundaries.

As the pain came surging out day after day, week after week, turning into months, I realized I was grieving much more than this lost love. I was grieving past relationships, I was grieving the loss of many, many friends to AIDS, I was grieving the multiple losses of my childhood, of the loss of my professional identity, of a happy, productive life in sobriety. I was mourning all the failures of my first forty years of life.

I was paralyzed with grief.

Les

It began to dawn on me that the brother I had feared and idolized for so long was no more than a thirteen-year-old boy with a cracking voice. I had blown up his power and strength into the size of a parade balloon, a huge darkening shadow that loomed over me everywhere I went. The beast I had carried in my mind all these years was no more than a kid.

I had stayed in the basement for twenty years, waiting for Brad to come back out of his room and make the pain go away.

That was never going to happen.

Eric I

I often wonder how I survived the first twenty-three years of my life. The last two, since beginning to deal with the effects of the abuse, have been so very different. There are days when the road seems too difficult and I wish I could go back to how I used to be: coasting, working, running, and *not feeling*.

Fortunately, and at times unfortunately, that is not possible.

I am really tired. Physically. Emotionally. Mentally. Every aspect of life seems to be a struggle for me.

I know there are many people out there in worse shape than I am. I should not feel the way I do. I should be able to overcome these downs and move on.

Right now it seems impossible . . . unreachable. . . .

It would be so much easier if I just died. I don't have the courage to take my own life. A combination of fear and guilt. So, once again, I dream of just dying a quick and painless death . . . something out of my control . . . something I can't be blamed for . . . but something that would end this pain.

For as long as I remember, I've had these thoughts . . . and this wish.

Nick

Faith and the ability to trust in general are common casualties of sexual abuse. Faith or belief in any sort of God or any richness or positivity in the life of the spirit are particular casualties—compounded when the boy's abuser somehow purports to represent the realm of the spirit. This is a particularly insidious abuse of power.

Recovery of belief in spirit and things spiritual are key to healing. The injury we suffered as boys was most of all to our spirits and our willingness and ability to believe. With recovered relationship with spirit comes open doors to connection and community with others.

Following my exit from the priesthood, I pursued graduate studies that earned me a degree in marriage counseling. I married in the early seventies and moved to Canada.

Since that winter of 1990, I have committed into writing the remaining pieces of the puzzle that had been missing. While some of these pieces, changes, experiences were traumatic and others very powerful they presented opportunities and invitations that I recognize as graceful. By being open, responding and integrating those experiences into my present life, I found myself gifted with an unexpected growth and overwhelmed at times with an inner peace of which I had not been capable before. Disclosure of the abuse to significant people in my life—my wife, children, trusted colleagues, family (mother is since deceased)—came easy.

Louis

Why I Am Not a Catholic

by Peter Murphy

I practiced communion for months, kneeling
at a cracked marble altar, my hands corrected by nuns
who squeezed my fingers into little shriveled wings,
turning them upward toward the starry ceiling
before laying a candy wafer on my tongue.
I prayed to the virgin's statue that looked down
in plaster silence, her bare feet crushing a snake's body
against a globe of the world.

Later, I was anointed by the priest
who wrestled me to the floor of the sacristy
and rubbed his hands over my body.
He massaged them into the joints of my spine,
pressed them into the muscles of my legs,
and stroked the soft flesh of my soul
which grew hard when he touched it, then died.

Nights, I knelt against my bed, reading psalms
aloud, chanting the dark words that flowed through me
like cold blood until you heard my wailing,
loved me for my sins and offered me your breast.
I did not believe I would ever come back to life,
but when you touched me and I rose toward heaven,
I was filled with tongues and could speak
for the first time the language of the living,
which gushed out of me in one intelligible voice,
ancient and beautiful.

The mind serves as a sanctuary during the arduous struggle to survive; feelings from the abuse are often a luxury the child cannot afford. Recovery and healing begin in the adult's life after he's realized both that he has now survived . . . and that he needs a whole different set of skills to live.

Movement into the realm of the heart is particularly scary; our resistance is entirely understandable. This is where we've locked up all the horror, rage, disgust, and pain at what was done to us as children. We wrap it all in determined detachment against the fear of ever trusting anyone with the power to hurt us like that again.

And yet, though it's never easy, recovery and healing require that we lovingly unwrap and feel it all, at our own pace, and willingly take the leap into trust once again.

Recovery is a slow and painful process. It is necessary to deliberately reach out to the child within me. The child who was unable to grow up, because that would have meant dealing with something that was too horrible to contemplate. I have to realize that it is "safe" now. I can remember this stuff and still survive. This means setting a lot of time and energy aside. The worst part is the raw pain that comes back with the memories. First I remembered the abuse with my mind. It took a couple of months before the full emotional impact hit home.

The process has its own schedule and I don't have a lot of conscious control over it. Moreover it is hard, in the midst of recovery, to know or see where I am. I rely on others to tell me if I am changing, and if so how. My emotions swing wildly from black depression and relative incompetence, to complete cerebral detachment and the emptiness that goes with it. Sometimes I am a lonely adult. Other times I am a vulnerable little kid. I seldom have any idea what is going to hit me next.

Murray

The multiple personality fragments into several distinct personalities, or alters, largely out of contact or dissociated from one another. This is an adaptive response to severe, and usually frequently repeated abuse. As we all do, the survivor who responds in this way needs to see and feel what's happened to him, and integrate his experience, in order to heal.

It blew him away. Hidden for twenty years, here it was. . . . Where did the brother's perversion come [from]? There was the dysfunctional family in which Billy was the weakest. There were mother and father who liked to use the belt and left the welts and verbally scared the child-soul. Here was what all the running had been from.

Therapy. Long hours tearfully trying to put back together the fractured child inside with the frazzled surviving adult. . . . More therapy, outpatient. Stabilization again.

But, before the shattered boy inside, Billy, and the man, Bill, could fuse, eight alters came out and Billy found out there were eight of him including: the Princess; the Masochist; the Mr. Nobody, who just wasn't there; the Mr. Competent, who had been gay rights spokesperson and AIDS activist; the Athlete, who ran marathons; the Governor, who ruled with a Southern accent and a stern hand pushing Bill into workaholism and overachievement;

Mr. Defeatist, who now took over for days alternating with Mr. Nobody. There were more. Were they all co-conscious? Did they all know each other?

Days at a time didn't exist. What day is it anyway? How do I tell? They came out and talked out loud to Bill now. They fought for control. They argued. Multiple Personality Disorder anarchy.

They were stunned into some kind of submission on the special unit of the hospital for Bill's fellow travelers, the abused and battered whose minds had also taken on multiple personalities to cope with the insanity. If each of the twenty-five of them on the unit had not been able to find the ESTian *it*, then each would have at least half a dozen alternate people to help with the search and with the hiding.

Eric II

Steps forward in recovery can be painful. The magnitude of the boy's injury and loss lives in the body's memory as well as the spirit's and the mind's. Touch remains confusing for the man, often either experienced as always sexual or avoided altogether.

I met someone at Al-Anon, a masseur. I told him I was a survivor and asked if he would help me with an experiment. I warned him that I would probably react. He came to my house. He was very kind and supportive. I lay down on his table. The moment he touched my shoulders I went into convulsions. I needed to see what this would do to me, but I had to ask him to stop. I just couldn't do it. Yes, I hate my father. I hate him more than I can say. I hate him for the loss of male friends, for the loss of touch and love, for the loss of the male me.

Mike

The watershed came when, in discussions with my (now sober) brother, I realized that we had both blocked out time when I was five and he was eleven. Having always had a "sense" over the years that I "might have been molested or something," I felt that our shared blocking was important. I began to attend a twelve-step program for survivors of childhood sexual abuse, I located an active, empathic, and skilled therapist and I began voluminous reading. I talked at length with my wife, whose perceptions of me are frequently more honest and less occluded than mine, and I also talked at length with my brother. From these efforts, I have begun to reassemble the story of my childhood as it really happened, not as I wish it had happened. My understanding of my childhood is an unfolding one, and I am far from done in my effort to understand what happened and how it affects me now.

I am becoming more willing to accept that I did not have a happy, loving childhood, that my childhood was harsh and filled with people who did not care consistently for or about me, both of my parents included. Accepting that my parents and the "shadow man" did not specifically care for me and, in my absence from their lives, would have simply acted out on someone else, makes it easier to accept that I lost my childhood well before I was grown.

Eric III

CHAPTER 13

MOVING ON

"SO, I CELEBRATE LIFE"

With some mysterious combination of love, luck, stubborn resilience, and plain hard work, we befriend our recovery process and make our own kind of peace with the past. We move on.

Healing is neither magical nor immediate. It is however rich, powerful, and hard work . . . and so much better than the alternatives. We direct our newly available energies into the present, the here and now, the man we've become today—through and because of and in spite of it all.

We are all still very definitely a "work in progress." Recovery is a lifetime job. There are always new levels and layers. Just as we each begin our own journey when we're ready, when we can, so too do we continue our journey toward wholeness at our own pace.

There is hope. I am gradually getting closer to that little boy. As I am able to experience more of his pain, I am able to bring more of him permanently into my consciousness and begin to integrate this long lost part of myself. People tell me that I have a bright future as a result of this healing. I have to believe them, but it is not a process that I can really control. Most of the time I go forward solely because there is just no alternative. It has been less than four months now since the first memories hit me. I am beginning to see changes in myself. But I suspect it may well be a long time yet, before I start to feel "normal," whatever that is. This is still very definitely a "work in progress."

Murray

I was going to tell him [my child self; in an imaginary dialogue] that even though we were going to hang up we could still talk anytime we wanted. I think I was going to say it to console myself, but as I sat on my bed I felt that it was true. I could still hear my younger self inside me very clearly. He was telling me he loved me too.

Eric I

I'm sad this journey of recovery has taken nearly fifty years but I could not have journeyed at all without the previous years. So, I celebrate life.

David II

In my personal therapies, in my work as a psychotherapist, now in its twelfth year, and as a graduate instructor in programs training others to become counselors and therapists, I have found myself spontaneously recovering lost parts of my past, and constantly challenged to heal more, integrate more, understand, and articulate it all to an extent I hadn't previously experienced. And I constantly find new layers and levels, keeping me humble, reminding me that this work is never fully completed.

Neal

As I visited my brother—a priest in the same order—a few months ago at the same house high up in the mountains of Italy, the echoes of a thousand memories from thirty years before, indelibly printed on my mind, were aroused in me. My life seemed as shifting, as uncontrollable, almost dreamlike to me during those days, full of shadows and inexplicable upheavals and transitions.

Then, I had been unsure that I could survive and function in a world so foreign to my normal existence. Now, I felt at home here; no longer threatened. It had been a terrible dream, but now all that lingers is the memory.

Louis

It can take awhile. It always begins by taking the first step. It gets better and better, little by little. You can learn to trust, yourself and others. You can touch and be touched and feel good about it.

You can invite children into your life with confidence and enjoy them (and they you). You can come to know, deep inside, that you are a good and worthy man, deserving of love—and that it never was your fault.

Some call this recovery, some healing. It's the alchemist's magic, the transformation of the baser in yourself into the finest into yourself. It can give you a whole new life, one you never imagined possible while still a prisoner of the abuse.

For the longest time, I have berated myself for feeling like a child inside. But, that's not right. The problem is, I've never felt like a child inside; what I've felt is fear and confused that with feeling childlike. I would like to feel like a child sometime, I think, now because I understand that can be different from feeling terrified to get out of bed.

A Survivor

In this past year I have begun a process of personal transformation, away from victimhood toward survivorship and a new life of freedom. To this day I am not free of the outrage and hurt I feel over this incredible betrayal of my soul and my personhood. My parents, and other adults in the family environment, robbed me of my life at a very early age. Today I know it is my right, my choice, my duty to myself to create and maintain emotional boundaries. I have a right to my wishes and desires, I have the right to say no and not feel badly. I have the right to not let other people hurt me. But I was nearly forty before I understood this.

As I write this I have been recovering for nearly two years. I am grateful that I have finally gotten to the bottom of the barrel of my problems, and that I have successfully identified it as incest and child abuse. I am profoundly grateful that I am alive, sober, sane, and healthy. I now know that many others who have been through what I have been through have been saddled with overt multiple personalities, paranoid schizophrenia, unchecked compulsive/obsessive disorders, unchecked alcoholism and drug addiction, and successful suicide.

I used to think of God, or my Higher Power, as just like the adults of my childhood—some benevolent-sounding, yet devious and sadistic monster that took relish in setting me up in order to knock me down, betray me, rob me of joy. Today I am learning to override that automatic discounting and self-blinding. I am beginning to trust that I have a right to be alive and to assert myself. It has been an incredibly slow and painful journey. The trauma is something I will always have with me. Having become aware of it and accepting it, I have finally been able to begin to do something about it.

I now live in Boston. I have a wonderful teaching position. I continue to grow and heal. I can reach out and work with others. I savor my personal autonomy. Someday I hope to develop a warm, loving, intimate relationship with a life partner, if I survive HIV long enough. Life is complex and full of challenges, and they are wonderful and exciting challenges. I am alive today. I am no longer a victim.

Les

A pirate came and robbed me of my childhood, of any love for men, for my father. . . . An adult who once could not cry now cries real tears and grieves the loss of a child.

S.K. Duff

One Christmas after I had resolved never to again see my father on Christmas, I stood in his living room as he proudly picked the local paperboy's card from his mantel to show me. I knew by my own dread, and the sudden emergence of a familiar paralysis of will, as much as by the exuberant glow surrounding my father as he spoke, that this boy was in danger.

The next week, in the process of filing a mandated report of sexual abuse in my clinical practice, I realized that while I was required legally to act in this professional context, I had a different, internal, requirement to act to protect my father's paperboy.

I called the appropriate police department in his town, and filed an anonymous report of concern against my father. The police believed me, the boy's family was alerted, and the boy was forbidden unsupervised contact with my father. I hadn't been able to prevent my own abuse, but I hoped I had done something positive for this boy.

The boy in me was very envious.

My father was arrested about a year later after two neighbor boys, ten and eleven, who he had tricked into his house, had fought him off and run from the house when he attempted to fondle them. The boys told their parents, who called the police. The boys' stories, taken separately, corroborated each other. The anonymous report on file offered further confirmation.

After a plea bargain and thousands of dollars in attorneys' fees, my father spent that Christmas, and his seventieth birthday, a convicted felon, in county jail, denying all wrongdoing.

The boy in me, again envious of the two boys was, at the same time, oddly gratified as I sat across from my father in the visiting room of the county jail. He was clad in a regulation orange jumpsuit; there was a thick glass between us, with guards on his side. I saw, for the first time, shame on that man's face as he looked up at me, holding the phone extension that allowed us to converse.

The adult in me was consumed with pity. This was an old man. This old man was my father.

Neal

I found comfort reading about other men coping with this loss of innocence and was utterly amazed that anyone else had ever had the same experience with almost the exact same emotional repercussions. I'm very lucky that I didn't turn to substance abuse or have a more violent or threatening abuser, but it's hard for me to imagine the day when I won't feel shame or guilt. I've come to realize that nothing will make the pain go away completely, or give me my childhood back, but I'll be damned if I'll let that bastard control one more minute of my life. . . .

I didn't really start feeling better until a few months into therapy when I dreamt that I went to a funeral. It was for me—actually I went to the funeral as an adult, because the funeral was for my childhood. There were the standard flowers, casket, card table, etcetera, in what first appeared to be a small chapel. My mother was sitting on the front couch reserved for family and I went over to her, collapsed in her lap and cried fiercely. She just held me and rubbed my back. It was the first time since she died that I'd seen her in a dream and she didn't disappear the moment I got near. As I sat up, I saw that it was not a small chapel, but quite a large room and everyone I know in my adult life was there to say good-bye to what I can't get back. It does feel like grief over who knows what could have been while I was growing up. It somehow closed the chapter on keeping the secret of my past and defining every thought and action since then against the experience of that monster. To those of you reading this book in search of some answers and forgiveness for yourselves, I can truly say, I've never felt worse, I've never felt better, but at least I'm feeling something, and am taking my life back. I hope you do too.

Gene

I had hoped to have the memories and scars removed completely.

Gradually, I have been able to incorporate this into my identity. Not in the self-pity sense. More like the Fisher King must first be wounded in the search for holiness. Somehow the membrane must be ruptured before healing can begin in the larger sense. Not just, "Stop the pain," but "How can the pain help me to help others?"

I am a new man. Wounded and maybe even crippled. But very much alive.

I bought five acres with a cabin that was a trash heap. As a daily spiritual task I labored picking up the debris by hand. I guess I was praying all the time. But it was late autumn and the ground was fairly bleak and barren. It didn't look like there was much life being uncovered.

Sort of like us survivors when help first arrives. We are lying dormant underneath somewhere. Not even conscious of a memory of having been beautiful.

So, like in any healing process, you just do the best you can. Then you leave it alone for awhile.

I drove the old Willys up the deeply rutted road one early spring day. I thought for a moment that I was on acid. There was a brilliant gold carpet of glacier lilies. They came up everywhere. Including the dry hard-packed ground. I sat down in the middle of it all totally rapt in awe. I was witnessing a miracle in nature that mirrored my own healing process. Those fragile bulbs had survived fifty years of abuse and neglect. But once the debris was cleared away, they came up everywhere.

I know there is healing magic in the touch. I know this is true for the two-leggeds and all other life forms. There are forces in the universe that perform miracles all the time. Wildflowers are one example of this. I am another.

C.L.

I searched my brain for the weight, the heavy feeling of the building, of the older boy's friend's father. The memory was there but the weight was gone. Not magically lifted, just real now, part of memory, part of a place and time long gone. In the telling of that story, the weight had become smaller, a small blue thing, that no longer lived in the present, on top of me inside of me, but in the past.

I knew it would never go away. But maybe it would get smaller. Maybe it would get so small that someday I could lay it inside a daisy just before it closed up at night. The last thing I thought before I curled myself around Mandy's body was that that should happen, the memory should get to go spend a night inside a daisy so that it could feel the softness and the warmth and the safety, so it could stop being afraid and stop making me afraid.

Robert

There's a Native American saying that goes something like this: The person who speaks with heart and with truth speaks with "spirit tongue." When our hearts find the courage to speak our truth, we too speak with spirit tongue. . . . We've begun to "climb the mountain" and our spirit has begun to find its rightful partnership with our soul. We begin to feel whole.

The shadow does gradually dissipate when our long-held secrets enter the light of day.

BECOMING THE ALCHEMIST

THOUGHTS FOR REFLECTION AND INSPIRATION

I once wrote a letter to my father attempting to confront him as an adult with what he had done to me as a child. This was an endeavor to communicate across the great divide between us that his incesting of me had created. I acknowledged that I had visited many worlds, internal and external, as a result of the abuse; worlds I might well never have otherwise known at all. He took this as absolution, which was not my intent.

I was trying to tell him I had done some alchemical work, had found a way to transform some of what he had done to me into something positive. I believe this is the process by which we all heal.

As we resurrect and reconstruct our personal truth, much as an anthropologist would in the physical realm, it can and does get better. We find that the depression lessens, a greater balance between good days and bad days comes gradually into being, and we actually start to like ourselves! We're one day aware that the quality of our relationships has improved; we find ourselves less alone in the world; we sleep better at night. Each time we tell the story, we heal a little more; when others who have suffered as we have hear our stories, they often are inspired to tell their own story, even if only to themselves, and they begin to heal or heal a little more. Healing "snowballs" and is contagious, feeding on its own momentum.

This is the fruit of the "alchemical stew" that Thomas Moore discusses at the beginning of the book. We can and must drink of this stew's "bitter juices" and transform the injury and the insult of our childhood sexual abuse into a golden wholeness, richness and depth in our lives as men.

Healing is this alchemical transformation's essence and fuel; it begins with speaking our truth.

What follows here are some passages for reflection and inspiration in the process of recovery and healing. These can be thought of as verbal snapshots of themes presented in the book, a place to turn for support and reminders in the path toward healing that we all share.

Healing involves the painful recognition that the sexual abuse of children springs from the shadow. It is an assault from the unconscious darkness of another, visited upon the innocent, that another might hurt as the attacker him/herself hurts. It's always much more about the abuser's pain and twisted need for power than it is about sex.

Healing is about restoring the spirit, the source of our play, our enthusiasms, our capacity to wonder, our hope and spontaneity, our very love of life. In many ways, all forms of abuse are injuries to the spirit much more than to the body. We need to heal our injured spirits.

Healing is a gradual process. We each are ready in our own time, in our own way, according to the wisdom of our own souls, to engage the arduous task of healing. We begin the journey home, we try to become whole, often for the first time, in putting together the shattered pieces of our inner lives.

Healing requires compassion for ourselves that we still need to be working on all of this. Issues of shame and boundaries and trust and patterns we thought long gone reappear, again and again. Healing and recovery is a lifelong relationship, an ongoing process.

Healing involves the recognition that our scars are deep and insidious; they stay with us for a very long time. Often, some interaction with others "reminds" us of some of our own wounds. This can be an important avenue to healing. We can come to know such reminders as gifts.

Healing requires going back and recovering, and then confiding, to ourselves and to others, the often awful truths about our personal history. It requires inviting, allowing, and bringing into consciousness what we've for so long needed to shut out.

H*ealing* means playing detective with our insides (territory a man is taught to regard as foreign, "women's stuff," to be avoided), a lifelong jigsaw puzzle of bits and pieces of memory, insight, emotion, and association. When we feel driven to put the pieces together, we know we've engaged the healing process.

H*ealing* requires grieving for all that wasn't, might have been and won't now ever be. Allowing our grief as men is key to freeing the injured boy.

H*ealing* needs help and support. As men today we need to surround ourselves with others who we can trust, who are safe so that we can risk being ourselves. This allows us to relearn vulnerability, this time as a strength, as something beautiful that enriches our lives and makes us better men.

H*ealing* means acting on what we know to be true, breaking out of the emotional paralysis with which our perpetrators have ensnared us. This includes embracing the confusion as a friend, entering into it in a fearless dance of determination to be free from it once and for all.

Healing means letting in all the feelings, no matter how much they hurt, how big they are, or how much they contradict one another. Foreign territory, again, for any male, gay, straight, or bisexual: we're conditioned to hunt, play ball, have a few beers, work some extra hours, "score" sexually, be right, be in control. This is not easy work for any man.

Healing means switching loyalties, from an internal enslavement to the perpetrator and the abuse to the freeing power of the truth, no matter how terrible.

Healing means finding, hearing, feeling, and believing the boy inside. He deserves it. He needs for us to find and reconnect with him.

Healing means coming to feel compassion for the child, for what has been done to us as boys, and surrendering the years of judgment and recrimination. We never were at fault. Our perpetrators did this to us.

Healing means claiming our rightful "home," inside ourselves and in the world; it means emerging from shameful isolation and zestfully joining into community with others as whole men.

Healing means trusting ourselves to find and know our own way. Each of us has his own course to follow to find the way home. None of us need be alone in the process. Like a child beginning to walk, we grow stronger and more confident with each new step—particularly when we know there's always someone there to catch us if we stumble.

Healing means claiming for ourselves as men our own definition of masculinity, of what it means to be a man. It means we can be rightfully proud of our struggles, our hard work, our integrity, and our selves.

You've survived, you're safe now; you're not alone.

SUGGESTED READING AND RESOURCES

Here are a few suggestions for the reader, for survivors and those who love them, who would like to explore this area more. We can all find additional information, affirmation, and support in these readings.

Listed first are some basic reading in this area, followed by some other readings that may also be helpful. The first six books contain exhaustive references and resources, including lists of organizations and newsletters, for the male and female survivor and their loved ones.

Lew, Mike. *Victims No Longer: Men Recovering from Incest and Other Sexual Child Abuse*. New York: HarperPerennial, 1990.

Hunter, Mic. *Abused Boys: The Neglected Victims of Sexual Abuse*. New York: Fawcett Columbine, 1990.

Bass, Ellen, and Laura Davis. *Beginning to Heal: A First Book for Survivors of Child Sexual Abuse.* New York: HarperPerennial, 1993.

———. *The Courage to Heal: A Guide for Women Survivors of Child Sexual Abuse*. Third edition. New York: HarperPerennial, 1994.

———. *The Courage to Heal Workbook.* New York: HarperPerennial, 1990.

Maltz, Wendy. *The Sexual Healing Journey: A Guide for Survivors of Sexual Abuse*. New York: HarperPerennial, 1991.

I also recommend these three volumes of men's essays, some of which speak directly or indirectly to the survivor experience, all of which are valuable reflections on the man's internal experience; and a book for men and women who want to rethink traditional ways of seeing men.

Abbott, Franklin, ed. *BOYHOOD, Growing Up Male: A Multicultural Anthology*. Freedom, CA: Crossing Press, 1993.

———. *Men and Intimacy: Personal Accounts Exploring the Dilemmas of Modern Male Sexuality*. Freedom, CA: Crossing Press, 1990.

———. *New Men, New Minds: Breaking Male Tradition*. Freedom, CA: Crossing Press, 1987.

Kupers, Terry. *Revisioning Men's Lives: Gender, Intimacy, and Power.* New York: Guilford Press, 1993.

For men and women who want to better understand the various dimensions of sexual addiction, and what can be done about them, I recommend the following.

Carnes, Patrick. *Don't Call It Love: Recovery from Sexual Addiction*. New York: Bantam Books, 1991.

And finally, for guidance and assistance in nurturing the essential realm of the spirit in oneself and in relationship with others, I recommend these two wonderful books.

Moore, Thomas. *Care of the Soul: A Guide for Cultivating Depth and Sacredness in Everyday Life*. New York: HarperCollins, 1992.

———. *Soulmates: Honoring the Mysteries of Love and Relationship*. New York: HarperCollins, 1994.